SELF AND COMMUNITY IN THE CITY

Jerome Krase
Sociology Department
Brooklyn College

UNIVERSITY
PRESS OF
AMERICA

HN
80
·N5
K7

PREFACE

This work reports on a small portion of my continuing sociological research on city neighborhoods. The subjects which are dealt with here are quite delicate and my long-term involvement in the community is both an advantage as well as a disadvantage for understanding and describing it. Although at first glance this may appear to be a case study of a single neighborhood, as in William Whyte's Street Corner Society, the abstractions and concepts either generated or employed in this piece are by no means limited to the particular site for this research. The same phenomena have been observed and documented by myself and others not only in American cities but cross-nationally as well. Sociological phenomena are seldom, however, expressed exactly the same way in any two locations.

The major theoretical theme of the book is the complex relationship between cultural symbols and societal structures which are embodied in the concrete entities of society--people, buildings, streets, maps and all forms of human settlements. One particular aspect of this general relationship is the interaction between self-images and the social meanings of the neighborhood communities in which people live. It is one of those many social phenomena "taken for granted" as part of everyday life and seldom analyzed, but nevertheless influential in the social construction of local community realities.

Although many social scientists have written about the relationship between the self and others, few have focused on the self-territorial community relation. George Herbert Mead had indirectly considered this relation of self and community in a discussion of William James and the question of consciousness. James had given an example of a person entering a house. The house has a history and the person who enters becomes part of its history. The house, simultaneously, becomes part of the person's history.[1] What I have done in this work is to attempt to synthesize the many ideas of self and

---

[1]George Herbert Mead on Social Psychology: Selected Papers, ed. with intro. by Anselm Strauss (Chicago: University of Chicago Press, 1964), pp. 65-82.

community from several disciplines and perspectives to form what I hope is a contribution to understanding this important dimension of human social life.

In general, the body of the text deals with examples of social and psychological meanings of human settlements, of self-image and the relations between them. I note that there is in society a tendency to balance the tension between self-image and the image of one's environment. The phenomenon is analyzed through the use of a Symbolic-Interactionist framework. The theories of cognitive balance and cognitive dissonance, developed by Festinger and Heider, are of course equally useful theoretical parameters for understanding and explaining this intricate process. The process is not limited, however, to the individual or group psychological levels. It also involves larger societal and cultural structures. The process is also dialectical in that individual self-images can change the image of the community and the image of the community in turn can change individual self-images. Ideally, we have a self-community feedback system which operates within larger social entities. Even the past and future are elements of the system exercising influence in the forms of history and expectations.

In many ways this report is also a personal sociological enterprise. Having had no outside support for the research is only one of several reasons for its obvious idiosyncracies. A central idea in this volume is the relationship between self and community images. A related concept is the parallelism between social mobility and geographical mobility. Erving Goffman has frequently reminded us of the importance of understanding social biography. As many others in our highly mobile American society, I am a person who has moved successively and success-fully over the past four decades from one neighborhood to another. This movement can be seen as an expression of personal socioeconomic advancement.

In my own case, the journey began in a low-income housing project in the notorious Red Hook section of Brooklyn. From there, my family graduated to a deteriorating tenement at the edge of Bedford-Stuyvesant. Our family served as janitors-in-residence in the building. We then moved through a series of Italian-American and Jewish middle-class areas after which I was off to a college dormitory in

Bloomington, Indiana, followed by Army barracks in New
Jersey, California and Frankfurt am Main, Germany.
After marriage in Germany, my wife and I lived in a
middle-class German neighborhood for two years and
then back to a married housing apartment park at
Indiana University. Upon graduation we returned to
Brooklyn and the setting for this book--Prospect-
Lefferts-Gardens.

When we came to the neighborhood we rented an
inexpensive "rent-controlled" apartment in the working-
class part of the community, not far from where my wife
was born and in which her parents and grandparents had
lived since the early 1900s. A few years later, we
purchased a home in the historically elite Lefferts
Manor section of the community. During this ten-year
span of time, the area changed from an "integrated" to
an essentially black community and is today the locus
of some "back to city" or "gentrification" activities.
Throughout our thirteen-year tenure in the neighborhood
we have been active in many local neighborhood associations and have personal as well as professional
interests in urban community dynamics.

Most of the issues raised in this work concerning
neighborhood change, ethnic succession and changing
self-images are therefore part of my personal biography.
However, this exposition should not be seen as merely
gratuitous. Karl Mannheim's discussions on the
Sociology of Knowledge caution the social scientist on
the importance of understanding the social position of
science and scientists in attaining maximum objectivity.
In a related vein, Max Weber considered the issue of
the social scientist as an activist, researcher and
teacher. He emphasized that a scientist must be able
to distinguish between what he sees in society and what
he would like to see. Both noted how one's values can
influence objectivity. With these thoughts in mind, my
remarks are intended to give the reader some benchmarks
from which to better evaluate this work.

As to whether or not this book is biased, I
would respond: "Of course it is!" No social product
is value-free. However, by making clear one's point
of view, the error due to bias is reduced. Being
political as well as social animals, sociologists
also have political orientations which effect the way
they see the world, the problems they choose to study,
their methods, the conclusions they reach and the
suggestions they make as possible solutions to

problems. For lack of a better label, I am a "pragmatist"; not only believing that there is a connection between how we think and how we act in society, but that we "ought to" act as we think. In this regard, my sociological research and writing parallel my civic activism aimed at reducing inter-group conflict and achieving the maximum degree of social and economic equality for all members of society.

If one denotes in my work a great degree of sociocultural equivocation, it can be assumed that it is not accidental. For example, I am less concerned with discrimination against one particular group in American society than with discrimination in general. Finally, I hope by this brief exposé that whatever errors the reader discovers in the text become as valuable as the "correct" conclusion at which I arrive.

One last point ought to be made about the purpose or intention of this book. It is granted that books are written for purely personal reasons --academic tenure, income, promotion, ego-gratification or having nothing else to do with one's time are equivalent in this regard. There are also altruistic reasons for publications. From my point of view, however, it is difficult to separate serving various communities, such as the professional and academic communities, from serving one's self. As a social scientist and a community activist, I have frequently criticized, from a safe distance and up close, the policies and programs of public and private agencies involved in alternately maintaining and destroying city environments. It is relatively easy to criticize when your own positions are not exposed to scrutiny. This work, I believe, makes clear my positions on many matters affecting city neighbor-hoods and residents. It also indicates some practical and theoreitcal approaches to community study and development which have been more or less ignored in prior efforts. I hope that the ideas presented here lead to further development and elaboration by others and that they may in some way influence the actions and attitudes of those empowered to maintain our urban environments.

ACKNOWLEDGMENTS

At this point I should take the opportunity to thank those persons, colleagues and community residents who were directly or indirectly helpful to the production of this work. First of all I must thank Charles R. Lawrence and Sidney H. Aronson for their confidence and support over the years; if not in my sociology at least in my humanity. Ronald Corwin gave me a start in the right direction and Edward Sagarin and Sylvia Fava reminded me at times where they thought I was going wrong. Alfred McClung Lee was a major influence in my humanistic vision of sociology. None of these aforementioned, however, should be blamed for the shortcomings of this work or of my personal sociology.

All the residents of Prospect-Lefferts-Gardens and Lefferts Manor and the organizations representing them are of course the supporting cast of this study. Special note must be made of the contributions and insights of the following, who may or may not agree with either my description or analysis of the situation: Henry and Kathy Broder, Michael Cetera, Elaine Ciccone, Frank Elcock, David Epstein, Henrietta and Anne Harris, Howard Jurgrau, Joe Kleid, Joseph and Sarah Kolb, Michael Leiman, Connie Lockley, Bob Marvin, Lillian Miller, John and Mae Morrison, Anthony C. and Rose Nicoletti, Alan and Sybil Oster, Alice Paul, Bruce and Ellen Raskin, Max and Helen Rosenberg, Mark Rosenblum, Bernice Sealy, Bob and Jane Thomason and of course my wife, Suzanne Nicoletti Krase. The Brooklyn College Foundation was generous enough to award me a grant for preparation of the manuscript, for which I am very grateful.

CONTENTS

CONTENTS (cont'd)

* * *

LIST OF TABLES, MAPS,
ILLUSTRATIONS AND FIGURES

LIST OF TABLES, MAPS AND
ILLUSTRATIONS (cont'd)

Chapter I

SYMBOLISM, SELF AND URBAN DEVELOPMENT

Ever since the establishment of permanent human settlements, a major concern of communities has been the defense of their territory. As villages and towns grew and their social structures became more complex, the necessity for defense against outside forces also increased, especially as the great cities came to represent competing empires, civilizations and economic interests. From the time of the ancient cities through the Middle Ages, the city was as much a fortress as it was a religious, political and commercial center.[1]

The advent of the Industrial Revolution and rapid technological advances in warfare shifted the focus of urban defensive postures away from external enemies inward toward the urban populace itself. Although modern cities no longer are encircled by thick walls patrolled by army garrisons, many of the neighborhoods within them are, so to speak, armed to the teeth, and invasions, successions, retreats and advances are quite evident on the urban scene. In many ways American cities, which are socio-economically, racially and ethnically diverse, continue a tradition of settlement warfare which stretches back to Neolithic times. From Los Angeles to New York City, crosses are burned, school buses are stoned and houses firebombed in attacks and counterattacks. Many more skirmishes take place in the courts and zoning agencies, but the primary battle zone lies within the minds of local community residents who are fearful of neighborhood change.

There is another kind of social and psychological contest taking place in American cities today the outcome of which may determine whether the spector of Necropolis that hangs over many of our urban areas is to become a reality. In essence, we as a nation must decide for ourselves if our dying and decaying urban centers are worth saving. If the current urban crisis is any indication of our national attitudes towards older cities, and I think it is, the decision has already been made in the negative.

1

The inner recesses of many older American
cities are at present remorselessly tormented places.
When we observe the actions of those empowered to
maintain the well-being of our urban areas, we see
that the methods they employ are like radical surgery,
without the use of anesthesia.   Over the past few
decades whole sections of cities have been obliterated by "urban renewal" without much regard for the
once living human landscape.[2] Other areas have
simply been cauterized by epidemics of arson and
neglect.   Still others are allowed to fester in
anticipation of future treatment,as, for example,
the "planned shrinkage" practiced in New York.   To
some degree the "Anti-Urban Bias" in American middle-
class culture helps to explain the triage biases of
urban planners, developers and other urban experts
toward their city and neighborhood patients.[3] Even
the current "gentrification" or "displacement"
processes that occur are not exceptions to this
general rule of symbolic warfare.   The middle and
upper-middle class gentry who take over select inner
city areas may be thought of as the troops that
occupy the territory after it has been scorched
and purged of undesirables.

It is obvious that the solution to many modern
urban problems requires the infusion of vast sums of
money, but the source of urban problems, which lies
rooted in the minds of people, will not be solved by
mere physical reconstruction.   Cities, and city
neighborhoods, must be seen as villages and small
communities are seen, as almost sacred human settlements deserving humanistic treatment.   One way to
effect change in the cultural perception of cities
in America is to provide urbanologists with the
conceptual tools for recognizing the positive and
negative, but nevertheless "human" nature of the
indigenous populations of inner-city neighborhoods.
For example, despite the alienation and sophistication
of modern society "History" is still venerated, as
witnessed by the current concern for the preservation
of historical landmarks.   Even the most debased of
inner-city neighborhoods have histories which can
provide a source for renewed vigor and perhaps
change the perception of them in the minds of
outsiders as simply collections of deteriorating
structures.

In order for history and tradition to have a
positive effect, it must be understood and appreciated

by neighborhood residents and those others, such as government agencies, who together control the future of urban areas. Toward this end "The Role of Symbols and History in Neighborhood Residential Succession" is emphasized in this work. The central practical argument here is that inner-city neighborhoods can be better maintained and improved by creating, and re-creating, the historically positive definitions and images of those communities.

The approach taken in this work should be referred to as "Symbolic Interactionist." In the past Symbolic Interactionism has been a relatively neglected perspective for research and theory in the study of urban social change.[4] As a theoretical perspective it has much to offer because it points out the role of symbolic definitions in the production of the social and physical decay that often accompanies neighborhood transition.

The process of residential succession, and the problems associated with it, have long been of interest to those concerned with the "urban condition." The phenomenon of urban residents symbolically interpreting and evaluating their social and physical environs has also been studied and discussed by many. Major works combining these aspects of urban social life span not only the dimensions of time and space, but also a wide variety of ethnic and social class groupings. Louis Wirth's The Ghetto (1928), Duncan and Duncan's The Negro Population in Chicago (1957), Anselm Strauss's Images of American Cities (1969), Gerald Suttles's Social Order of the Slum (1968), and Herbert Gans's Urban Villagers (1962) are a few of the important contributions to the areas of community transition and community symbolism.[5]

Despite the fact that an abundant literature on urban social life presents a ready-made opportunity for the development of a Symbolic Interactionist theory of urban deterioration, little has been attempted toward this end. In particular, Walter Firey's pioneering work on "Sentiment and Symbolism" as major factors in the social and economic value of urban real estate in Boston, and Gerald Suttles's conceptualization of the "defended neighborhood" have not been fully exploited for their potential value.[6] One reason for this neglect is the common assumption that symbolic approaches must be limited to monographic, or other purely descriptive tasks. Social policy is

3

not seen as a symbolic matter. As qualitative
studies, often employing participant-observation and
other "soft" methods, symbolic studies are often
matter of factly dismissed as sociological novels
with more literary than scientific value.[7]

Symbolic Interactionist, phenomenological or
other qualitative approaches to social life are,
however, not merely methods to provide access to
subjective social worlds for artistic display. The
participant-observer is no ordinary voyeur. To the
qualitative social scientist, subjective social
contents affect and influence larger scale objective
events. One of the best arguments for the study of
ordinary people's subjective experiences was
classically stated by Max Weber:

> Sociology is a science which attempts the
> interpretive understanding of social action
> in order thereby to arrive at a causal
> explanation of its course and effects. In
> "action" is included all human behavior
> when and in so far as the acting individual
> attaches a subjective meaning to it. Action
> in this sense may be either overt or purely
> inward or subjective; it may consist of
> positive intervention in a situation, or
> of deliberately refraining from inter-
> vention in a situation. Action is social
> in so far as, by virtue of the subjective
> meaning attached to it by the acting
> individual (or individuals), it takes into
> the account the behavior of others and is
> thereby oriented in its course. (1966:88)

Moving out of or into a neighborhood, abandoning
an apartment building or setting it afire, vandalizing
public and private property, all are "social" acts.
The symbolic perspective helps to re-establish the
connection between the minds of inner city residents
and their environment. Using the perspective in
regard to urban policy, one must argue that this
connection exists in a causal as well as a philosophical way. Often policy experts take the position
that knowledge of the subjective experiences of city
residents is of little value in explaining urban
problems. The micro-social level of life is buried
under the weight of macro-social and economic factors
responsible for the decline of cities. A more
humanistic vision of urban life would show that the
ordinary city dweller's experiences and feelings are

4

important sui generis.[8] Furthermore, even if the feelings of ordinary people about their local environment are of little value in explaining what has happened to American cities, this situation in itself should be of great interest to urbanologists. What does it mean for a city when the study of the attitudes and values of its residents is a sociological waste of time? How is a city structured to account for the practical irrelevance of the opinions of its citizens?

These questions, in various forms, should be the central theme in the humanistic study of modern urban society. The tools for analyzing the personal dilemmas of city residents have been provided in the studies of social and psychological alienation by Sigmund Freud, Georg Simmel, Karl Marx and David Riesman, among many others.[9] Unfortunately, social scientists today seem to be more concerned with measuring and objectifying alienation of urban residents than with seeking to understand and eliminate it. C. Wright Mills lucidly describes the problem of modern alienation and argues that making sense out of our confusing existence is the goal of the "Sociological Imagination." The persons that Mills describes below are accurate theoretical portraits of inner city residents who try to come to grips with an environment that often seems to be incomprehensibly crumbling around them:

> Nowadays men often feel that their private lives are a series of traps. They sense that within their everyday worlds, they cannot overcome their troubles, and in this feeling, they are often quite correct: What ordinary men are directly aware of and what they try to do are bounded by the private orbits in which they live; their visions and their powers are limited to the close-up scenes of job, family, neighborhood; in other milieux they move vicariously and remain spectators. And the more aware they become, however vaguely, of ambitions and of threats which transcend their immediate locales, the more trapped they seem to feel. . . . Seldom aware of the intricate connections between the patterns of their own lives and the course of world history, ordinary men do not usually know what this connection means for the kinds of men they are

5

becoming and for the kinds of history-
making in which they may take part. They
do not possess the quality of mind essential
to grasp the interplay of man and society,
of biography and history, of self and world.
They cannot cope with their personal
troubles in such ways as to control the
structural transformations that usually
lie behind them. (1959:3-4)

As in the past, symbolic and related writings
today tend to be polemics of the scientific and
political dehumanization of modern people. On the one
hand, human beings, especially city people, are
increasingly being defined in non-human terms (e.g.,
consumers, producers, etc.), and on the other, the
power of ordinary people in cities to have significant impact on their communities has become
theoretically and practically problematic. The
scientific dehumanization of social subjects has
been promoted by the works of Konrad Lorenz, Robert
Ardrey, Desmond Morris and more recently Edward O.
Wilson and Stanley Milgram.[10] In urban and neighborhood study, human activity in reference to physical
space is often equated with the territorial activity
of lower forms of animal life, implying that human
and animal communities are analogous--the city is an
ant hill, and the ghetto a jungle.

The potential value of symbolic interactionist
theory as an antidote to the dehumanizing treatments
of urban social worlds comes from the fact that it has
a democratic, humanistic, ideological basis. The
relationship between its ideology and its theorizing
is described here by Leon Shaskolsky:

The writings of the symbolic interactionist
are permeated with an exhilarating optimism--
expressing itself, on the personal level, in
the belief in the uniqueness of each member
of society and in his freedom to perform his
everyday actions in interrelationship with
others unencumbered by either the impinging
rules of a structural society or the
automatic responses of an uncontrolled
personality; and expressing itself on the
societal level, in the belief in an evolu-
tionary process of change built into the
system. Not for Mead a Sumerian jungle
favoring the fittest, but a society

6

undergoing gradual change and held together
by the empathetic understanding of inter-
acting individuals. . . . Mead's accent on
the individual was one of respect and under-
standing--not the right to forge ahead at
the expense of others, but the obligation
to have regard for the other in "defining
the situation": to take the role of the
other in order to determine the other's
expectations; to play out, through meaningful
gestures in conjunction with others, life's
changing situations. (1970:17)

One would have to agree, humanist or not, that
modern cities dehumanize people and that citizens are
having less and less power to control their own lives
and situations. Ultimately, the strongest argument
for a symbolic study of urban neighborhood life is
the overwhelming power of extra-local, super-
community entities to define and control the local
scene. Roland Warren defined the social community
as "that combination of social units and systems which
perform the major social functions having locality
relevance. This is another way of saying that by
'community' we mean the organization of social
activities that afford people daily access to
those broad areas of activity that are necessary
for day to day living" (1972:9). By a process of
elimination, community study at the local level has
become the study of what ordinary people think about
what happens to them, and how they successfully, or
vainly, strive to psychologically mediate their
environment.

Indeed, the power of larger social entities to
influence local people even in their personal evaluations of their own neighborhoods is a major problem.
The mass media and educational institutions play major
roles in this process by conditioning people to compare
their local surroundings with American suburban middle-
class standards. Anyone familiar with televised or
printed advertisements for non-urban residences could
not help but to agree on this point. Also, one need
only request that an inner-city child draw a picture
of "house" to see the pointed roof, chimney, and
trees which are part of a cultural, artistic and
aesthetic vision of the American "home" and
"community." These and other dominant cultural
standards of community lead large numbers of inner-
city dwellers to negatively define themselves and

7

their environments, which are usually far from aesthetically pleasing. Relatedly, Kenneth B. Clark and others have shown how dominant cultural values related to personal appearance have influenced the psychology and self-image of minority group members. This problem is epitomized in Clark's study of black children which showed that they preferred light skins, and thereby demonstrated a degraded view of self.[11] Herbert Gans similarly noted in his work, People and Plans (1968), the biases of urban planners and policy makers who evaluate working-class neighborhoods according to their own professional middle-class values, often leading to the destruction or disruption of viable urban communities.

A thought-provoking view of the effect of self- and community images is given here by Malcolm X in his Autobiography:

> So I went gawking around the neighborhood--the Waumbeck and Humboldt Avenue Hill section of Roxbury, which is something like Harlem's Sugar Hill, where I'd later live. I saw those Roxbury Negroes acting and living differently from any black people I'd ever dreamed of in my life. This was the snooty-black neighborhood; they called themselves the "Four Hundred," and looked down their noses at the Negroes in the black ghetto, or so-called "town" section where Mary, my other half-sister lived.
> What I thought I was seeing there in Roxbury were high-class, educated, important Negroes, living well, working in big jobs and positions. Their quiet homes sat back in their mowed lawns. These Negroes walked along the sidewalks looking haughty and dignified, on their way to work, to shop, to visit, to church. I know now, of course, that what I was really seeing was only a big city version of those "successful" Negro bootblacks and janitors back in Lansing. The only difference was that ones in Boston had been brainwashed even more thoroughly. They prided themselves on being incomparably more "cultured," "culti-vated," "dignified," and better off than their black brethren down in the ghetto, which was no further away than you could throw a rock. Under the pitiful

misapprehension that it would make them
"better," these Hill Negroes were breaking
their backs trying to imitate white people.
(1964:40)[12]

There is a definite relationship between the
powerlessness of ordinary neighborhood residents,
their alienation, their images of self and the images
they and others have of their neighborhood. Understanding these connections may make clearer the
frustrations of people involved in inner-city community organizations. Because local residents have
minimal formal authority to control their environment,
even when formal organizations develop out of shared
sentiments on the local scene the groups are, with
few exceptions, ill-prepared and virtually powerless
to do more than attempt to delay or quicken the
inevitable through what are best seen as cathartic
community rituals. Examples of these rituals, that
are almost expected in today's cities, are the
pathetic demonstrations and community rallies which
stand out sharply from the otherwise untribal performances which take place on the city streets.
Planned or spontaneous community performances are
analogous to the activities of teenage street gangs
who try to defend their "turf" from outside enemies.
It should be noted here that the "Amboy Dukes" of
Brooklyn's Brownsville were ultimately incapable
of keeping their community from being taken over
by nonwhites.[13] Whereas in the decade of the sixties
we saw community protest primarily in minority, low-
class areas of the city, analyzed by the Kerner and
other commissions,[14] we see in the seventies and
shall see in the eighties, a growing trend of
community-based protest in white middle- and upper-
middle income areas. The suburbs are also not
immune to protest against changes that affect
community definitions, as noted by the hostility
toward making low-income housing available in suburban areas and the integration of suburban schools.
All these community protests, from riot to demonstra-
tion, deal in some way with how people define and
feel about the neighborhoods in which they live.

It is hoped that some of the discussions in
this book will also provide the basis for a better
understanding of the tenacity of some urban neighborhood residents to preserve and protect their
communities, and conversely the willingness of others
to destroy them. This is of particular importance

today given the well publicized predictions of the inevitable physical and social deterioration of the nation's cities, which was once limited to Northeastern regions, but now is expected in all areas of the country including the "Sun Belt." The consensus on this point of eventual decay is so broad that by contemporary common-sense definition, inner-city, transitional and decaying neighborhoods are synonomous terms.

A statement which demonstrates this taken-for-granted notion of inner-city hopelessness was given in 1967 by Eleanor Wolf and Charles Lebeaux but is just as relevant today. Not only did they see the inevitable devastation of inner cities, but suggested strategies for combatting it as well.

> By now everyone is aware of those changes in the population of the central city which have combined with a number of other factors to create the current concern about American urban life. In the pages that follow we will examine two kinds of responses to the so-called "crisis of the city." First, we will consider the efforts to halt, reverse, or otherwise exercise some control over the population trends of the city so that it will not become overwhelmingly the abode of disadvantaged people. We might describe these as efforts to affect the spatial distribution of "haves" and "have nots." Second, we will examine some of the present trends in our efforts to improve the situation of the poor, especially those efforts usually categorized under the heading of social welfare programs, but including education. (1967:99)

It is not difficult to understand how this widely accepted vision of the present and future lives of cities is instrumental in the society-wide, self-fulfilling prophecy of urban decay. One primary element in this vision is the equation of nonwhite habitation with urban deterioration.[15]

Residential Succession: How "Losers" Win

The usual methods for studying the phenomenon of urban neighborhood residential succession are

generally ecological in orientation. These methods
emphasize the necessarily commensal relations
between potentially competitive groups in regard to
residential space, and other local territorial
objects such as streets, parks and stores. Historically, the opponents in these urban territorial
contests have been defined in ethnic, racial,
religious or social class terms. Some, also, as
Wolf and Lebeaux have done, employ "have" and "have
not" terminology. The data for ecological studies
are most often drawn from decennial, special and
other census reports, and is sometimes supplemented
by independent demographic surveys. Ecological
studies of residential succession in inner-city
neighborhoods most often arrive at the illogical
conclusion that "losers win," that is, lower status
and less powerful groups, over time, conquer
contested areas. The earliest studies of residential
succession in American cities focused on European
immigrant groups such as Eastern European Jews,
Poles, Irish, and Southern Italians. Since about
1940, succession in the city seems to be a scenario
in which blacks, Hispanics and other non-European
ethnic groups are the major characters who battle
entrenched "whites." Increasingly, in cities such
as New York the traditional black-white confrontations
are being augmented by a melange of black, white,
Asian, Middle-Eastern and Hispanic contests over
local territory. There has also been some intra-
ethnic group rivalry as well; for example, Carribean
vs. American blacks, Cubans vs. Puerto Ricans, etc.

Although both "common knowledge," and generaliza-
tions from "scientific" studies of urban residential
succession similarly argue that the people who invade
city communities tend to be of lower socio-economic
status than those whom they ultimately defeat and
replace, logic should lead us to question this
scientific folklore of city life. Besides logic,
there is also a growing array of data that disputes
the point. Some of the most interesting contradictory
data concerning the social status of traditional
black invaders is here provided by Taeuber and Taeuber
from their important work, Negroes in Cities:

> Turning to the characteristics of Negroes
> living in Invasion Tracts and Negro Areas
> in the six Northern and border cities, two
> general observations may be made: (1)
> Negroes in invasion tracts are of higher

11

educational and occupational status, are
more likely to be homeowners, and less
likely to be crowded than Negro Areas.
Movement into previously all-white areas
is clearly led by high-status Negroes.
(2) Negroes in invasion tracts are often
of higher educational status and more
likely to be homeowners than whites in
these tracts, both before and after
invasion. Not only are high-status
Negroes the first to enter all-white
neighborhoods but owner-occupancy is
apparently a major avenue of entry into
the new neighborhood. That incoming
Negroes are not of higher occupational
status than in the white population reflects the fact that Negro occupational
levels are not consistent with their
levels of educational attainment, in
large part because of job discrimination.
. . . These findings support an obviously
plausible supposition that high-status
persons of whatever color tend to seek
out the best available areas of
residence. (1965:163-64)

Negro Pioneers and White Flight

At least one major case study of residential
succession involving blacks argues against the common-
sense assumption of the lower status of invading
blacks who come into white neighborhoods. Northwood
and Barth found that "Negro Pioneers," especially in
the first wave of invaders, tend to be of higher
socio-economic status than their white neighbors.[16]
One must realize that the first blacks into a white
neighborhood will have higher hurdles placed in their
way than for incoming whites. Blacks will pay
higher prices for homes, and, in general, be "more
selected" and "acceptable" to dominant whites in the
area. The invasion even of exceptional blacks into
previously all-white areas does, however, result in
symbolic effects that may eventually change the
socio-economic, as well as ethnic, character of
the area. Experience shows that "integrated"
neighborhoods become "nonwhite" neighborhoods
over time.

It appears that only after a variable "Tipping Point" is reached does an area seem to take a general socio-economic downturn. To most scientists the tipping point is a simple proportion of non-whites to total population in the area, after which the area slowly or rapidly becomes essentially all non-white.[17] In symbolic terms the tipping point is the degree of stigma, or preponderance of negative definitions associated with non-white invasion, that changes the neighborhood from one that is contested to one that is uncontested. In other words, at some point whites lower the barriers for non-white invaders, and lower status invaders are allowed to pour, or trickle, in. It is at this symbolic juncture that the rapid deterioration of a neighborhood can take place.

This process of stigmatization of a community, and its expected advent, contaminates all those who occupy the stigmatized territory. At the "tipping point" the non-white pioneers join their earlier antagonists in contemplating, or actualizing, flight from the area. This results in a sort of hesitating or sporadic flight rather than a steady exodus, and is more typical of actual neighborhood change. The study at hand, which focuses on the symbolic elements of neighborhood succession, should lead to a more reasonable explanation of the physical and social deterioration that has been correlated with non-white movements within the nation's inner cities, urban, fringe and, in the future, suburban areas.

The delayed flight process from contested areas is one of the complicated social and psychological phenomena that are likely to be obscured by urban studies based on decennial census data. In my own experience, and those of others who have intensively studied changing inner city neighborhoods, it appears that non-white pioneers of high status and lower status late arrivals are seldom separated by more than four or five years. Many of the families I have met, for example, have been "pioneers" two or more times within a decade and have subsequently fled from "changed" city neighborhoods.

Given the wide-spread practices in the real estate industry of racial steering, block-busting and other sales-producing tactics, the pace of racial turnover can vary greatly; most often it

comes in surges. Therefore, reliance on decennial
data can result in erroneous conclusions about the
process of change in a neighborhood. This problem
is in addition to the notorious inaccuracy of small-
scale census data, and information collected in nonwhite urban areas.

There are other aspects of residential change
in the inner city that require more intensive study.
For example, a slow rate of home sales in an area
can still coincide with a high rate of ethnic
change. Often non-white invaders are the only
prospective buyers, and whites the only sellers,
of neighborhood property. Many of the residential
blocks I have researched in the city had rather
"normal" turnover rates; approximately four percent
per year, but due to racial steering by white and
black real estate agents during a ten-year period
they shifted from being predominately white to
being predominately black. On these residential
streets there was no "panic," which is the common
picture presented of invaded areas. Perhaps for
the word "invasion" should be substituted "occupation"
as a term to describe change in these communities.
Such a change in terminology might also help to
reduce the inherent bias in research on changing
communities.

An additional factor that tends to increase
the perception of rapid change in contested areas
is that non-white invaders tend to have more members
in their households, which more quickly reverses
racial population balances in a community. Often
larger black families replace older single or two-
person white households. Invading non-white adults,
being younger than dominant whites and having
children who are likely to play on the streets,
also tend to be more "visible" in the community.
The degree of perceived ethnic change in an area
becomes even greater than the real numbers would
prove it actually to be.

Relative Selectability among Minority Invaders

Most of the problems created by the "normal" ecological approach to urban neighborhood study, which
emphasizes demographic analysis, are the result of the
view that social science should be as "naturalistic"
as possible. Leon J. Goldstein states that a

naturalistic social science is " . . . a social science which takes as its point of departure not the living experiences of members of a society, but, rather, the questions that the investigator thinks are worth answering" (1965:88). Because of the methodological and theoretical biases of those who take the naturalistic approach, the residential movements of lower status minority groups in American society are treated as though they were part of a natural process completely controlled by the severe limitations placed on their options for residential location. Naturalistic social scientists are especially interested in the macrological processes and events that are beyond the control and even the everyday experiences of ordinary people.

This approach makes absurd the suggestion that a researcher, such as myself, should ask people about the "why's" and "wherefore's" of their residential movements. I suggest on the contrary that much can be gained from such investigations. The undeniable fact of institutionalized housing discrimination in America obscures the differential degrees of housing options within minority poulations, and between those groups who are universally discriminated against. One cannot seriously argue that light-skinned blacks have the same degree of difficulty being accepted by white neighbors as those of ebony complexion, for example, or that there is some measure of difference between the housing choices afforded to upper and lower income minority group members. One would assume that such naiveté concerning racialism was demolished by John Dollard's study of Class and Caste in a Southern Town (1949) and other reports on the complexity of American racial, ethnic and religious bigotry.[18]

Middle- and upper-middle class minority group members, socialized well to hold American middle-class values, do attempt to locate themselves and their families in neighborhoods that reflect, or support, their claims of social respectability. We might even argue that for them the visible symbols of middle-class status are even more important than for middle-class whites who take their situation more for granted. Despite the fact that middle-class non-whites are a minority within a minority, the greater economic and social advantages of these "elites" increase the residential options available to them. This statement is not intended to over-

gloss, or to downplay, the extreme problems of
housing discrimination for American non-whites, but
to differentiate the locational problems of higher
status individuals from those of lower class minority
group members. These class-related differences in
housing location and lifestyle are apparent in the
classic studies of white communities such as Whyte's
Street Corner Society (1943) and the Lynds'
Middletown (1929).19 Unfortunately, modern
social scientists choose not to see differences
within minority ethnic groups, perhaps for ideological reasons.

There are then, within and between racial and
ethnic groups, relative degrees of selectability of
neighborhood and type of dwelling accommodations.
There are also central residential and housing values
in American culture which are transmitted to all
members of the society. These community values are
a part of what may be termed a general (although
not exactly universal) "culture of community" in
America. Structurally, and naturalistically, all
members of society are provided with various degrees
of access to, and financial ability to attain, these
housing and community goals. As with past white
European invaders into occupied city neighborhoods,
today's better-off non-white invaders will tend to
occupy the best possible areas of restricted residential space. Even within this more "open"
territory presented to them, such as deteriorating
inner-city areas, they will locate in the most
desirable sections of those areas, as compared to
the less powerful and less advantaged members of
the same ethnic group. When living in the same
neighborhood with less advantaged cohorts, the
elites will occupy the more valued and prestigious
accommodations as noted by National Urban League
studies.

Although all these social facts can be understood in normal ecological terms, the symbolic
perspective offered in this work makes more understandable the processes involved in locating people
in particular neighborhood community settings. It
also helps explain why some locations and types of
dwellings are more desirable than others, and leads
one to consider the processes by which socially
valued meanings, which can increase or decrease
the attractiveness of neighborhoods, are learned,
discovered, transmitted and used to evaluate one's

community, and relatedly, one's social and psychological self. In the end, it is these processes which can also foster neighborhood stabilization or its unfortunate deterioration.

Symbolic History and Self

Considering the great contributions of George Herbert Mead, Charles Cooley and other social psychologists concerning the creation and continuous development of the social self, we should be led to entertain notions of the effects of inhabiting socially meaningful territories on individual and collective psyches.[20] To elaborate: how does it affect one's self-conception to be able to say to a "significant other" that I slept in the same house as did George Washington? What does this mean for the people who are like me? What does my act of sleeping there, and the others like me who have done the same, express and communicate to society? Am I better or worse off for the experience? Why should I feel honored to have lain there? How does this occupation of historically meaningful territory influence my personal identity, and by extension the identity of the groups to which I belong? Along these same lines, in recent years, American ethnic groups have been increasingly concerned with their "roots." Many make pilgrimages to the historical sites that are part of their group identity. For example, middle-class blacks take trips to Africa, and also visit slave quarters in the South. For many people the trip to venerated territory, the ethnic Mecca's and Jerusalem's, has an enabling effect. Realizing the social and psychological value of territory and property, one can see how these values become part of the necessarily conspicuous and expressive consumption of urban residences that has been an integral part of all ancient and modern civilizations. Did not the upper classes of Ancient Rome covet the neighborhood of the Palatinate? Do not presidential candidates have a desire, not only to be President but to sleep in the White House? Residences have always had important social meanings. This social reality is not restricted to America and Italy; one need only think of the symbolic values of places like Number 10 Downing Street, the Kremlin, the Taj Mahal and Peking.

17

Neighborhoods and homes are physical and symbolic entities which have both official-objective histories and symbolic-subjective ones as well. The understanding of why and how people move into or out of a neighborhood (or a whole city for that matter) can be only enhanced by information concerning the symbolic meanings of places and their residential histories. Also of importance are the processes by which these meanings are created, discovered, learned and communicated. Such knowledge should help us to understand, and perhaps predict, the future of particular or general types of residential communities.

Consider the common experience of meeting someone who, in the process of identifying himself or herself, proceeds to tell you where they live. The information that their talk conveys to you is much more than simple geographic coordinates. People do not tell each other the longitude and latitude of their home. We live in suburbs, exurbs, cities, small towns, ghettoes, good neighborhoods and bad ones as well. We live near, or with, the notable and the notorious. Why do many people tell others about the famous people who have lived near them? Our surroundings, as a dramatic setting, are believed to "give off" information about ourselves. Our residence attests to, or belies, our claims of particular social status and prestige.[21] We may hide negatively meaningful facts, and highlight and advertise positive ones. In sum, we can be stigmatized or celebrated for our address.

One of the foremost examples of especially meaningful urban residential location was provided by President John F. Kennedy in 1960. On a trip to accentuate the United States' political and moral commitment to freedom and the NATO alliance, he chose to deliver his major speech in West Berlin; then widely thought of as a symbolic anti-totalitarian community. His pledge to defend Berlin, which symbolized all American allies, was punctuated by the statement: "Ich bin ein Berliner," and he was resoundingly applauded for the symbolic gesture.

The meanings attached to particular residential areas are shared only by those who also share similar socialization experiences and knowledge. For example, to be "ein Berliner" in Tel Aviv, certainly will not

18

automatically result in crowd appreciation. Within
America there are many neighborhood names which have
wide symbolic currency; Harlem, The French Quarter of
New Orleans, Greenwich Village, the South Side of
Chicago and the Gold Coast, as well as Watts, Boston's
Roxbury and Hollywood,are a few examples of "familiar"
neighborhoods. More abstractly, ethnic neighborhoods
are often referred to as "Chinatowns," "Harlems,"
"Little Italies," and "El Barrios." Not too long
ago, most large American cities had areas referred
to as "Jewtowns." The economic and subsequent
geographic mobility of America's Jewish population
seems to have quietly eliminated the term from
common usage, only to be replaced by references to
Jewish suburban communities as "Gilded Ghettoes."[22]

There are international symbolically meaningful
neighborhoods as well: Paris's Latin Quarter,
London's Soho, Tokyo's Ginza and North African
Casbahs have meanings that are widely recognized by
educated people in all parts of the world. Neighborhoods then are not simply places on maps or on the
surface of the earth; they have mental locations as
well.[23] It is therefore not unreasonable to expect
that, if given a choice, knowledgable people will
try to locate themselves in residential settings
that they feel will adequately, or more than
adequately, compliment and enhance their own ideas
about self, and the ideas held by others about them.
Naturally, people who think well of themselves will
try to convey the most positive information about
themselves to "significant others."

One's residence is not necessarily a "truthful"
representation of individual social worth. People
who live in crime-ridden slums are not necessarily
"bad" people, but they are nevertheless socially
degraded for their address. On the other hand those
that occupy city "Silk Stocking" areas are not always
respectable and substantial. An example of the use
of an address for devious purpose was provided to me
by a janitor at a luxury apartment building on
Manhattan's Sutton Place, an extremely exclusive
neighborhood. He related that often there were
several tenants in the building who, in his words,
"didn't belong." These were people trying to
"make it big" in New York and needed an address
that would impress business contacts. Some would
lavishly furnish apartments through credit arrangements and also throw expensive parties for

impressionable guests. Others had virtually no
furniture and simply picked up their mail at the
apartment house and answered telephone calls. If
these people would fail in their financial dealings,
as they usually did, they would "skip town" without
paying rent and other bills. The "ethnic" politician
who maintains an address in his district while living
in the suburbs, or a more luxurious neighborhood,
similarly uses residential symbolism in a devious
way.

It seems appropriate at this point to provide
some general outlines of a theory of the relationship
between neighborhood community and self-image. First
we ought to be familiar with the common assumptions
and propositions of Symbolic Interaction as a
theoretical perspective, here provided by Arnold
M. Rose:

> Assumptions:
> 1. A human being lives in a symbolic world.
> 2. A human being is stimulated and
>   stimulates others with symbols.
> 3. A human being learns through symbolic
>   communication.
> 4. Symbols and their meanings and values
>   frequently occur in complex clusters
>   such as roles which guide the individual's
>   behavior.
> 5. A human being's ability to think permits
>   an assessment of his course of action.
>
> Propositions:
> 1. Human beings can predict each other's
>   behavior and adjust their own behavior
>   about their predictions.
> 2. Human beings define themselves in
>   relation to other persons and situations.
>
> (1962:3-19)[24]

Georg Simmel, who had a significant impact on the
style and direction of American urban sociological
enterprise, notes here from his essay, "The Metropolis
and Mental Life," the struggle of the urban individual
to find meaning for "self" in the confusing urban
environment:

> Here in the buildings and educational
> institutions, in the wonders and comforts
> of space-conquering technology, in the

20

foundations of community life, and in the
visible institutions of the state, is offered
such an overwhelming fullness of crystallized
and impersonalized spirit that the personality, so to speak, cannot maintain itself
under its impact. On the one hand life is
made infinitely easy for the personality
in that stimulations, interests, uses of
time and consciousness are offered to it
from all sides. They carry the person as
if in a stream, and one hardly needs to swim
for oneself. On the other hand, however,
life is composed more and more of those
impersonal contents and offerings which
tend to displace the genuine personal
colorations and incomparabilities. This
results in the individual's summoning the
utmost in uniqueness and particularization,
in order to preserve his most personal core.
He has to exaggerate this personal element
in order to remain audible. (1950:422)

To Simmel's ideas I might add that one's home
and one's neighborhood are two of those "personal"
elements that urban dwellers can use to express their
uniqueness and their distance from others while amid
the masses. As stated by Suttles:

Like the family, the neighborhood is largely
an ascribed grouping and its members are
joined in a common plight whether they like
it or not. . . . Perhaps the most important
of these structural elements is the identity
of the neighborhood itself. A neighborhood
may be known to be snobbish, trashy, tough,
exclusive, dangerous, mixed or any number of
things. Some neighborhoods may simply be
unknown and reference to one's residence
may arouse only puzzlement and necessitate
one's explaining one's guilt or virtue by
residential association. In any case,
neighborhood identity remains a stable,
judgmental reference against which people
are assessed, and although some may be able
to evade the allegations thrown their way,
they nonetheless find such evasions
necessary. (1972:35)

Elaborating on this relationship between self and
residential environment, Alvin Schorr has argued that:

21

To the middle-class reader, the social elements that are involved in identifying himself with his housing may be evident. These are the common coinage of deciding where to live. Who is accepted there? Are they my kind of people? It is a step up or a step down? What will it do for me and my children? Whom shall I meet? The physical elements of self-evaluation may not be so evident. Indeed, it has been suggested that our culture tends to put out of the mind the deep personal significance of what has been called the "nonhuman environment." It is interesting and perhaps also just that psychoanalysts are among the first to bring back to our minds a relationship that more primitive societies understand. (1970: 320-21)[25]

In an important essay which mixes architecture with Jungian psychology, Clare Cooper has written of the house as a "Symbol of Self" (1974). In this brilliant and insightful piece she describes the relationship between a person's dwelling place and how that individual sees him or herself <u>vis-à-vis</u> others, and a cosmic universe. She emphasizes that this relationship has cultural and political ramifications. For example, she notes that in Anglo-Saxon law, the person and the home are considered to be inviolable entities. This psycho-cultural emphasis on the equation of property with personal rights is carried over into American civil and criminal law as well.

She goes on to note that people tend to choose homes, and to decorate them (exterior and interior), in fashions and styles that the inhabitants feel adequately display their individual and collective identities. This psychological process, according to Cooper, takes place at both conscious and unconscious levels. The unconscious aspect of these residential choices, she finds, can be shown in an analysis of dreams of occupants. In support of her propositions, Carl Wertheim in a study of housing choices, concluded that many people bought houses which they felt would bolster their self-image both as a unique person, and as an occupant of a certain status position in society (1974:132).

If we combine Cooper's psychoanalytic notions of self-home with Vance Packard's research on American cultural norms regarding social mobility, reported in A Nation of Strangers (1972), it is easier to understand the social pressure that people feel to make their neighborhood surroundings conform with the estimates they have of their own social worth. Packard also found that status seeking promotes a great deal of residential movement in America, which can result in a reduction of the strong traditional ties to any particular place. On the other hand, this striving also increases the concern of residents about the social value of their community. Residences, as jewelry, clothing, cars and school ties, are symbols of relative prestige.

In reference to changing urban neighborhoods we should expect that when any area suffers a reduction in its symbolic social value, or when its historically sacred meaning is lost or tainted, then people who live in them will seek out other settings in which to locate themselves. These settings would more adequately reflect their image of self. Alternately, people will be attracted to, or remain within, communities that they believe have high symbolic social value. People who are forced to remain, or who simply have no opportunity to move out of "profaned" community settings will subsequently suffer a concomitant loss of self-esteem. Those that choose to remain in a defiled neighborhood setting will experience social and psychological conflict between self and community images, and may feel compelled to engage in activities which would reduce in some way this cognitive imbalance.[25] This dilemma is cogently and ironically demonstrated by the comic strip segment of Motley's Crew in Illustration 1.

Symbolic History: Modern and Ancient Foundations

Up until this point, I have been occasionally critical of "normal" urban community research, especially that which is ecologically and demographically oriented. There is ample justification for such criticism, but there are also many other good reasons for employing normal methods in this and other studies. The concern I have with the usual techniques of urban community research is not their propensity to err and to misinterpret, but that unless they are combined

23

Illustration 1.   THE PSYCHOLOGY OF BEING "LEFT BEHIND."

From The New York <u>Daily News</u>, October 1, 1976: 60.

with other more sensitive data-gathering techniques,
and more subjectively oriented disciplines, one can
never obtain a complete and useful picture of the
urban social reality. This reality, because of its
extreme complexity, requires multi-method and multi-
disciplined approaches.

The general theory of the relationship between
self and community, and the particular case of
symbolic residential succession presented here, is
an example of such a theoretical and methodological
marriage. One aspect of this theory of residential
succession is that "symbolic history" is often the
key to understanding the housing choices of invading
groups, who move into contested middle-class areas
of the inner city, and the eventual fate of the
changed area.

The use of local history in the sociological
analysis of urban neighborhoods has a long tradition
itself. Robert E. Park, one of the most important
figures in urban sociology, stressed in his work that
local history and local traditions are necessary
components of the definition of urban neighborhoods.
He stated in The City that neighborhoods begin as
mere geographical units but over time become localities
with sentiments, traditions and histories of their own
(1966:3).

Relatedly, from an anthropological perspective,
the universal relationship between locality and
culture is made here by Conrad M. Arensberg and Solon
T. Kimball from their Culture and Community:

>   Communities seem to be basic units of
>   organization and transmission within a
>   culture. They provide, for human beings
>   and their cultural adaptation to nature,
>   the basic minimum of social relations
>   through which survival is assured and the
>   content of culture can be passed on to the
>   next generation. Already pan-animal as
>   ecological units, communities are pan-human
>   as transmission units for human culture. It
>   is their function, in keeping alive the
>   basic inventory of traits and institutions
>   of the minimal personnel of each kind for
>   which culture provides a role and upon
>   which high-culture specialization and
>   acceptance can be built, that makes human

25

communities into cell-like repeated units
or organizations within human societies and
cultures.

We can rely, then, on this hypothesis for
ordering the experience of American communities we will cite. Without defending it
further, we must notice at once that it
implies that each culture has its characteristic community which serves as such a unit
and that each isolatable type of community,
as such a unit of cultural organization and
transmission, stands for an isolatable
culture. We can hypothesize a one-to-one
correspondence of some kind between culture
and community. (1965:97-98)

Neighborhood communities, then, have general
societal as well as particular histories, traditions
and cultures. It is within this complex situation
that the individual urban neighborhood residence is
found, and ultimately must be understood.

Søron Kierkegaard argued that history is no mere
collection of facts but the interpretation of events
by people who fill those events with meaning.[27] In
this work I emphasize the duality of objective and
symbolic history. To use my earlier example for
purpose of discussion, the fact that George Washington
slept in a particular place is an historical (objective) event, but the fact that someone is "proud" to
sleep in the same place implies that the event has
symbolic, and possibly mystical, value. The meaning
of an event does not automatically follow from the
datum of Washington's choice of lodging. Historical
fact and social meaning are separable. The meaning
of an historical event, as well as the event itself,
can influence the current and future social actions
of individuals. Predicting or understanding the
action that ensues because of, or in regard to,
historical events must be based on accurate knowledge
of the symbolic content of the event, and not only on
knowledge of the event as a naturalistic occurrence.

To elaborate on the above point, whether or not
George Washington actually did sleep in a particular
location is less important to understanding social
action or psychological feelings regarding that
place than is the symbolic meaning of that event as
a reasonable "possibility." One might only assume,
or have been told by an unscrupulous innkeeper, for

example, that he spent the night in this place, when actually he did not. People tend to act on the basis of what is known to them, and not on what is unrevealed. In order to understand the impact of symbolic meanings, and their resultants in action, individual and collective social selves and their store of historical knowledge must be known.

Social selves are the products of largely standardized, collective, socialization processes, but they are also shaped by idiosyncratic socialization events. From people with similar socialization experiences we should expect similar reactions to symbols. We might hypothesize that an under-educated or non-American person would not be eager, or even willing, to spend a larger sum of money to sleep where Washington (it is alleged) had rested his weary head, if offered equally comfortable accommodations. American history buffs and tourists would be most likely to compete for such shelter. They are also the ones most likely to boast of their "meaningful" experience to others who would appreciate it.

Fixed places inherit meaning from hypothetical events, but meaning and symbols are more mobile and transportable than the fixed place, and the restricted temporal setting. The event of Washington's slumber in a particular bed, in a particular house, etc., does not preclude the desirability of sleeping in the same bed in a different room, and so on. One can ask higher prices from appreciating buyers from reproductions of America's first President's furniture, than for those of his contemporaries who are of lesser renown. Whole historical periods and their representations ultimately have meaning and social value. Antique collectors constantly discuss the relative merits of Colonial, Federal and other style periods. Finally, history itself has general value, and is similarly sanctified and mystified.

It is interesting to note that the veneration of historical figures and events has today resulted in a growing number of urban activists who cite historical values as sufficient grounds for halting "urban progress," which often comes in the form of demolition of "old" buildings and neighborhood reconstruction. In New York City the efforts to preserve historically valuable structures and

neighborhoods are centered in the New York City
Landmarks Preservation Commission. Similar agencies
exist in other cities and counterparts can be found
at stage, regional and national levels. The New York
group has the authority to grant "landmark," and
other lesser statuses, to buildings and areas of
the city that meet their strict criteria for
historical or architectural notability. These
designations tend to prohibit, or limit, the power
of property owners to alter their homes or other
physical structures without prior approval of the
Commission. The Commission represents the formaliza-
tion and bureaucratization of urban historical
symbolism. The actions of the Commission also
represent the particular social values of American
society in choosing what is, and what is not,
worthy of preservation. Why, for example, do
commissions concerned with general historical
values tend to preserve the homes of wealthy
industrialists, and not those tenements which
had cloistered their equally important work
forces?[28]

   What does the value of history and sacred
meanings have to do with neighborhoods, cities and
urban society? Why is it important for the so-called
experts of city life to be aware of symbolic history
and its relationship of self-identity? To answer
these questions, it is necessary to understand that
an urban neighborhood, as any other kind of human
settlement, from tribal village to high-rise
apartment house, is not merely a geographic and
physical entity. Fustel de Coulanges, in The Ancient
City, described the historical and mythical founding
of Rome. On the day of the founding a sacrifice
is offered. The founders light a fire of brushwood,
and leap through the flames. De Coulanges's
explanation of this rite is that in order to participate in the act people must be pure, and primitive
people thought they could cleanse themselves by
jumping through a sacred fire. According to the
myth, Romulus then dug a small circular trench and
threw a clod of earth brought from the city of Alba
into it. Then each of the companions followed his
example and threw in some dirt from the place from
which they came. The rite reveals the mystical
and symbolic ideas of ancient people. Prior to
Rome they had lived in other cities such as Alba.
In those cities were their own sacred fire and the
ground where their fathers had lived and were buried.

Their religion prevented them from leaving the land where their hearth was located, and where their divine ancestors rested. Therefore, each man had to carry with him a clod of earth as a symbol of the sacred soil of his ancestors to which their manes were connected.

> This rite had to be accomplished, so that he might say, pointing out the new place he had adopted, This is still the land of my fathers, terra patrum, patria; here is my country, for here are the manes of my family. . . . When placing in the trench a clod of earth from their former country, they believed they had enclosed there the souls of their ancestors. These souls, reunited there, required a perpetual worship, and kept guard over their descendants. At this same place Romulus set up an altar, and lighted a fire upon it. This was the holy fire of the city.
> Around this hearth arose the city, as the houses rise around the domestic hearth; Romulus traced a furrow which marked the enclosure. Here, too, the smallest details were fixed by a ritual. . . . As the plough turned up clods of earth, they carefully threw them within the enclosure, that no particle of the sacred earth should be on the side of the stranger. This enclosure, traced by religion, was inviolable. Neither stranger nor citizen had the right to cross over it. . . . But in order that men might enter and live in the city, the furrow was interrupted in certain places. To accomplish this Romulus raised the plow and carried it over; these intervals were called portae; these were the gates of the city. (1975:136-37)

Modern cities and neighborhoods are not less tradition-rich than ancient ones. However, there is the common moral conviction that modern cities are far more profane than sacred, but all human settlements have founders, foundations, rituals, myths and customs. Even the decimated Brooklyn neighborhood of Brownsville was once a village founded with a vision to provide decent housing for people who would work in nearby factories and shops.[29] Modern citizens are perhaps less observant and reverent than were their ancestors, and perhaps the meaningful past is less apparent and less appreciated by the large number of uninformed, desensitized urbanites who inhabit most cities. The majority of the ordinary residents of city neighborhoods have little knowledge of the rich history of their locality, or even of their political urbis. Often those that are historically informed act as though they were heretics, showing no respect for the past. Irregardless of this common situation there is a great deal of recent, and more distant, history that has had effect and continues to affect the welfare of current city neighborhood communities. Also, people forget that their own contemporary experiences are historical; what happens to them in their life time is inexorably connected to other prior and future events.

In many ways the founding, eventual decline, and desecration of Rome is analogous to the rise and fall of many of today's urban neighborhood communities.

Chapter II

SELF SELECTION AND URBAN DECAY

Beginning in the 1960s and continuing through the 1970s, American society seemed to be at war with its largest and oldest urban areas. In some cases whole cities have succumbed to intensive attacks on their social, economic, environmental and political bases. As the smoke of battle clears, and for some cities the haze is just beginning to clear today, not only isolated ghetto neighborhoods, but large portions of the nation's once vital and energetic urban centers can be seen to lay in ruin. Some observers have compared these desolate urban landscapes such as the South Bronx in New York with Nagasaki, Hiroshima and the bombed-out European cities at the close of the Second World War.

Over the past ten years I have walked the streets, during the daylight hours, of the devastated sections of many American cities as well as those of my own New York. Having been stationed with the United States Army in Frankfurt am Main during 1964 and 1965, I was made personally aware of both the scars of wartime bombardment, and of the possibility of building upon ruins. I must admit that the view of burned-out hulks of buildings in American inner-city neighborhoods have troubled me more than those war scars in Germany. Throughout history, major cities, and other centers of civilization, have been obliterated by man-made and natural disaster. Leipzig in 1941 was no less damaged by bombs than was Pompei by a volcano; but to understand the destruction of Pompei one needs only to understand Nature, and Nature needs no motives for what it does. To fathom the devastation of London, Dresden, Phnom Penh or Jonestown, it is human society and the people who comprise and influence it that must be analyzed. The internal wars waged in modern American cities were, except for the urban riots of the 1960s, less dramatic than military tactics used against European and Japanese cities. Our own urban warfare is, however, more interesting because it is far less comprehensible.

31

The difficulty in understanding today's extensive urban blight stems from the apparent cooperation not only of government agencies and powerful interest groups, but of the city's indigenous peoples who assist in the destruction of their own communities. In many cases the spread of deterioration takes on an almost epidemic and suicidal pall. For some, urban decay in the form of arson is cause for celebration as witnessed below:

> The flames dance high as heat bites into old woodwork, searing and twisting the wooden frame until it gives in floor by floor, wall by wall. Condemned to death by the living, the abandoned building on East 4th Street burns madly. A couple of Molotov cocktails carefully ignited and carelessly thrown light up the block as hundreds of local residents mill about, singing and dancing, having a good time. An impromptu block party. In their faces can be seen the last power left to poor people. Fire power.[1]

The mass self-destruction of Masada, as Jewish residents chose oblivion rather than surrender to the Roman siege, is a polar version of modern urban neighborhood negation. There, Jews sought to preserve their social integrity through mass suicide. The ruins of slums will not be memorialized. In large measure the social and economic problems of American cities are caused, and accelerated, by decisions of millions of middle-class people to abandon their homes and neighborhoods, while fleeing for the "better world" of the suburbs. These ex-urbanites are somehow convinced that the places in which their own families had lived for generations are not worth saving, or maintaining. The city is "not good enough" for them. So they leave, and with them they take their money, their skills, their education and their political power, creating a vacuum that is soon filled with the less fortunate. America became over the last two decades a suburban nation. The urban middle class in the inner city, and some fringe areas, were replaced by the poor, the disadvantaged and the disenfranchised. This mass migration accentuated the self-fulfilling prophecy which continues to echo: "The cities are dying."

The loss of the urban middle class is essentially a function of what is often called "White Flight." In New York City it reached such crisis proportions in 1975 that the New York City Commissioner of Human Rights Eleanor Holmes Norton (herself black) publicly predicted a "Dim Future for City if White Exodus Continues." In a widely reported news release, she noted that between 1970 and 1975 the minority (nonwhite and Hispanic) population survey showed that between 1970 and 1973 the city's white population had decreased by 8.3 percent, or from 4.9 to 4.5 million people. At the same time the black population had increased by 5.6 percent and the Hispanic by 11.5 percent.[3] All of these facts led the Commissioner to openly state that "We [New Yorkers] have a very good chance of being in the situation Newark is in by 1980."[4] The 1980 Census showed that the white exodus continued.

Articles such as these cannot help but to make the problem worse, for bad publicity about city environments and prospects convinces more people that the time to move is "now." They also add credence to the common-sense belief that blacks, and other non-whites, equal urban blight and disaster. We shall see in later pages that this equation is a major factor in the creation and spread of neighborhood deterioration by which nonwhites paved the way for bulldozers.

There have been many books and articles written, and research studies conducted, which have attempted to describe and explain what happened to American cities since the great exodus of white and middle-class families began. My work differs only in focus from these other contributions. You might say that it is an attempt to describe and explain what might have happened versus what actually did happen in at least one inner city neighborhood: Prospect-Lefferts-Gardens. The story of this community belies the assumption that the disease of urban blight is a purely natural and inevitable phenomenon.

New York City, always in the forefront of developments in urban life in America, shared the unenviable position of leader in urban decay with many cities of lesser renown. Harlem and the Lower East Side in Manhattan, the South Bronx, Bushwick and Brownsville in Brooklyn today compete in

33

notoriety with Newark, Watts, Chicago's South Side, Boston's Roxbury and East St. Louis. All these neighborhoods have become household words which arise in discussions of what is wrong with modern cities. The Borough of Brooklyn, as a whole, may soon have the opportunity to be added to the infamous list of urban failures, as deterioration spreads from the desolate confines of low-income ghettoes into middle-class communities. Map 1 indicates those areas in 1969 which were considered severely deteriorated. Over the next ten years the major change was the gradual increase in the area of blight.

As shown in Map 2, Prospect-Lefferts-Gardens is located in the center of Brooklyn. Close by to the north is Crown Heights, and slightly beyond is Bedford-Stuyvesant. Crown Heights gained some fame in the 1950s via the actions of "Maccabees," a group of Orthodox Jewish men who patrolled neighborhood streets with clubs in an effort to stem the tide of a growing number of muggings and robberies. In 1978 and 1979 vigilante activities, in Crown Heights and elsewhere in New York's changing communities, splashed across newspaper front pages once again. Although at first deplored by public officials and seen by many social critics as a temporary unique aberration, vigilante groups are now a national phenomenon. Crown Heights, besides being the home of the Lubavitcher Hassidim, is also reported to have a very large population of legal and illegal Carribean immigrants who work in basement sweatshops and crowd into dilapidated apartments. Bedford-Stuyvesant, the largest black community in America, is struggling to recover from the almost complete ruin of the 1950s and 1960s. To the east of Prospect-Lefferts-Gardens are East New York and Brownsville, large minority communities depopulated by fires and urban renewal. There, as in parts of Bedford-Stuyvesant, huge tracts of open land where once homes and apartment houses stood are slowly being reforested. In many places in Brownsville hardy urban tree varieties and shoulder-high weeds completely hide the underlying rubble.

Each day several more houses and buildings burn to the ground in Brooklyn, and arson is an almost daily occurrence, for fun, profit and revenge. In Brooklyn's low-income ghettoes Fire Department officials complain that their men are pelted by stones and bottles (sometime they are also shot at)

Map 1. MAJOR ACTION AREAS IN NEW YORK CITY, 1970.

■■■■ Major Action Areas
* Crown Heights

Source: Critical Issues Volume, Plan for New York City, 1969.

From <u>CHAMP Facts</u>, 1972: 52.

Map 2. BROOKLYN NEIGHBORHOODS.

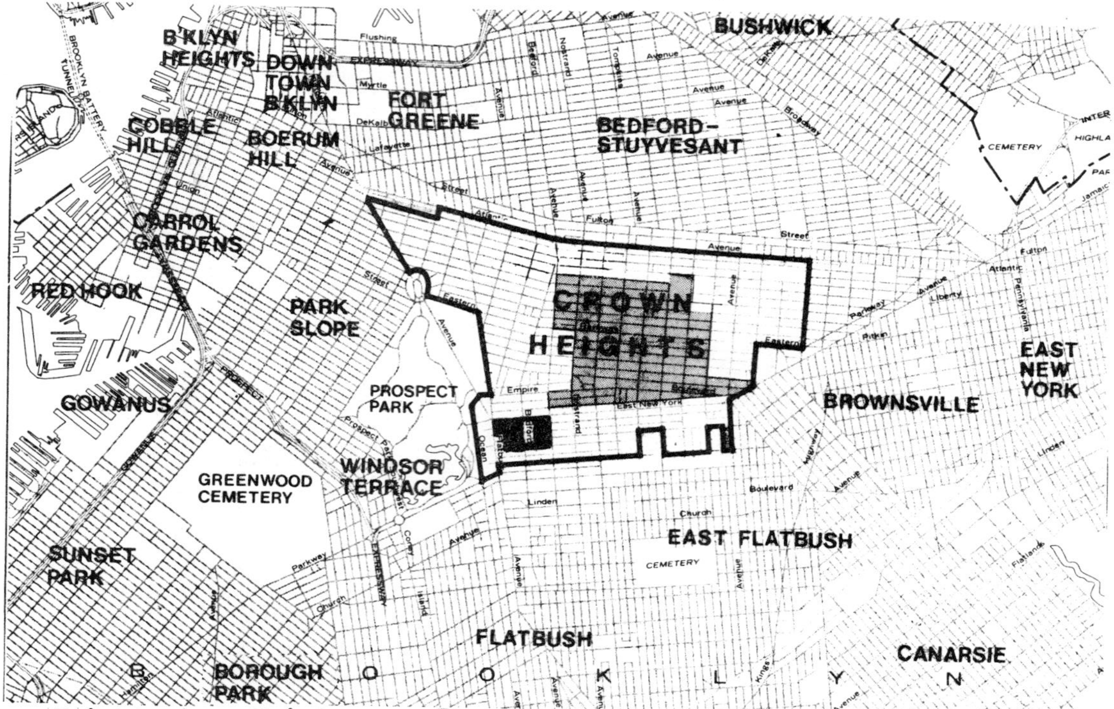

Crown Heights Area Maintenance Program

Prospect-Lefferts-Gardens

From CHAMP Facts, 1972: 17.

36

thrown by neighborhood residents. At times, firemen
are escorted by police as they respond to alarms.
Today, the well-known Flatbush area of Brooklyn is
experiencing the first phases of urban blight;
commercial street deterioration, mortgage red-
lining and increasing crime rates. Most worrisome
of all is the decreased confidence of residents
that their community will be able to survive much
longer.

Although the general picture of Northern and
Central Brooklyn has been bleak, even in the middle
of extensive decay one can find a small number of
residential neighborhoods which have effectively
resisted deterioration, and are "surviving." These
inner city anomalies, most of which are exclusively
black middle-class communities of one and two family
homes, offer a glaring contrast to images of the
inner-city ghetto neighborhood. It is hoped that
by understanding the conditions which exist in
"surviving" areas, and the processes which have
taken place in them, that we will be better able
to combat the spread of urban blight into other
communities in New York and other cities.

Prospect-Lefferts-Gardens is located in the
southwest corner of New York City Community Planning
District 8.[5] CPD 8 is one of sixty-two such
districts, ostensibly created by the City Planning
Commission in 1960 to facilitate the decentralization
of city services and political control. These
districts are shown in Map 3.

Although there are many extant analyses of the
decentralization phenomenon in New York and other
American cities, it is the affective and ideological
values associated with this decentralization that
are here the most interesting.[6] As expressed by the
then Mayor John V. Lindsay:

> The plan I am proposing would establish a
> single Community Board for each Community
> Planning District in the City, with full-
> time staff, community offices, and a
> Community Cabinet of local city officials.
> This plan provides for one local body to
> deal with all city problems, with a broadly
> based membership and the capacity to monitor
> effectively local services. It can end

Map 3. BROOKLYN'S COMMUNITY PLANNING DISTRICTS, 1975.

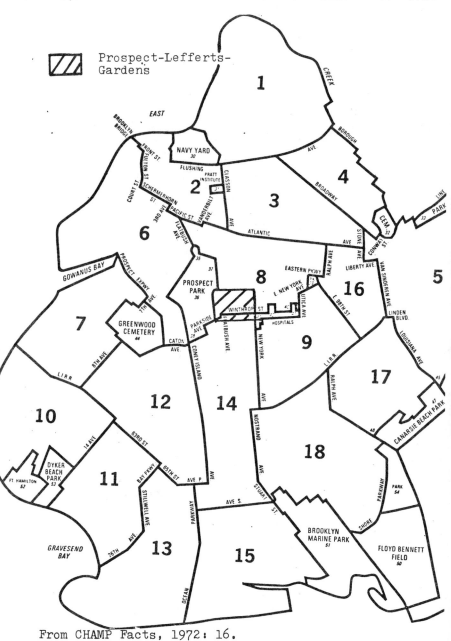

From CHAMP Facts, 1972: 16.

duplication, broaden citizen involvement, and make city government more accountable to the communities they serve.[6]

The original boundaries for the districts were adopted by the City Planning Commission in 1968. Most of the boundaries have remained stable over the years, but those for CPD 8 were recently changed to reflect the political differences between the black political powers of the Bedford-Stuyvesant area and Orthodox Jews in Crown Heights. Such ethnic and political differences will continue to loom larger and larger as the Community Planning Boards themselves are given greater powers and service responsibilities as called for by the recently revised New York City Charter.[7]

From the outset, the districts were intended to be "meaningful" communities, at least from the perspective of the delivery of muncipal services. Topographical, economic, social, historical and political boundaries were all taken into account when drawing up the present lines for the Districts. Despite the planning that went into the formulation of the CPDs, the original District 8 was far from being a homogeneous community. Part of this problem is that these "Community" Districts tend to be extremely large in population. For example, in 1960 CPD 8 had a population of over two hundred thousand people, greater than many American <u>cities</u>.

Because this study emphasizes the changes in the center of Brooklyn over the years, the original Community Planning District Boundaries will be used as reference points. Within the boundaries of the area there are many distinct neighborhood communities that have very little in common with one another. These neighborhood communities range from the Lubavitcher Hassidic community of Crown Heights, to the Haitian immigrant community a few blocks away, and from the upper-middle-class black neighborhoods of Bedford-Stuyvesant, to nearby low-income housing projects. Also, the landscape of the area offers scenes that range from large urban parks, to block upon block of burned-out ruins.

The community district arrangement does, however, provide some advantages for the urban researcher. Principal among these assets is the compilation of census and other information on an

area-wide basis. This situation allows us to
compare the experiences of specific neighborhoods
with the general conditions of the District and
makes it easier to chart larger scale demographic
changes.

Table 1 shows that during the 1960 to 1970
decade the District had changed from one that was
predominantly white, to one that is predominantly
nonwhite in racial composition; in 1960 CPD 8 was
seventy percent white, in 1970 it was seventy
percent nonwhite. In 1980 it is nearly ninety
percent nonwhite. Prospect-Lefferts-Gardens, in
the southwest corner of the District, was in 1970
considered to be on the leading edge of the nonwhite
migration southward across Brooklyn, yet in 1970
it was still sixty percent white. By 1980 the
neighborhood is close to eighty percent nonwhite.
The reasons for this slower rate of racial turnover in the Prospect-Lefferts-Gardens neighborhood
are both cause and effect of the lesser degree of
physical deterioration in the area.

The acceleration of the racial turnover
between 1970 and 1980 was related to the differences
in tenancy of white and nonwhite populations in 1970
as shown in Table 2. Then, the basically middle-
class black residents lived in local houses zoned
for one and two-family occupancy. Others lived in
the large number of small multiple-family dwellings
on the major thoroughfares running north and south
through the neighborhood. The white population was
concentrated in the high-density, large apartment
houses which were successful for many years "keeping
out" nonwhite tenants. A large proportion of the
white population in these buildings were older,
single and two-person households. Younger, more
afluent tenants began to leave in large numbers in
the early 1970s, and today most of these buildings
are almost exclusively nonwhite in composition,
with a smattering of aged, poor white tenants.
This situation seems to be a common characteristic
of changing neighborhoods in New York City; apartment houses resist change for a longer time, but
change more rapidly once the racial barrier is
breached.

These and other demographic and ecological
features of the Prospect-Lefferts-Gardens neighborhood are in themselves fascinating, as well as the

Table 1. POPULATION BY ETHNICITY FOR CROWN HEIGHTS
AND PROSPECT-LEFFERTS-GARDENS, 1960 AND 1970.

	1960	1970
Crown Heights*		
Total	206,076	216,924
Nonwhite	63,185	161,345
White	142,891	55,579
Prospect-Lefferts-Gardens		
Total	25,272	25,469
Nonwhite	2,464	13,779
White	22,808	13,779

*Figures are for Community Planning District 8. For
comparability in 1980 Census figures for Community
Planning Districts 8 and 9 must be combined. It should
be noted here that Community Planning District 9, as
presently constituted, contains a higher proportion of
White residents than does District 8 from which it was
severed. The bulk of the White population in District
9 in 1980 consists of a large community of Hassidic
Jews, four of five blocks north and to the east of Prospect-Lefferts-Gardens. There is also a substantial
undercount of the Black population, given the presence
in the District of large numbers of undocumented workers
from Haiti and other Carribean countries.

Source: United States Census of Population, 1960 and
1970.

Table 2. TENANCY BY ETHNICITY FOR CENSUS TRACT 798*, 1950, 1960, and 1970.

	1950	1960	1970
Total Housing Units	3,124	3,147	3,748
Owner Occupied	281	326	308
White	278	231	149
Nonwhite	3	95	159
Renter Occupied	2,806	2,799	3,407
White	2,795	2,778	3,071
Nonwhite	11	21	336

*Census Tract 798 was chosen for this table because it is the most representative of Prospect-Lefferts-Gardens. Most of the owner-occupied housing exists within the Lefferts Manor. As noted in the text, the great potential for ethnic change in the community comes with the change in the composition of the large apartment houses which up until 1970 had resisted the integration which had occurred in the single-family home sections of the community. Although, at this writing the 1980 Census data is not available by tract, it appears that over 90 per cent of the tenants in the Renter Occupied Units in Tract 798 are at present nonwhite. This represents a radical transformation from 1970.

Source: U.S. Census of Housing, 1950, 1960 and 1970.

numerous community organizations that have developed
over the years to both foster and retard social
changes in the area. However, it is not the changes
in the community that have been most apparent and
intriguing, but the things that have remained the
same. It is generally assumed that a necessary
feature of ethnic and racial residential succesion
in the inner city is the rapid decline of the invaded
area as evidenced by increased social and physical
decay. One expects crime, deterioration, housing
abandonment and other problems to expand drastically.
It is also expected that the class and physical
structure of the community will change.

     Initially, Prospect-Lefferts-Gardens did not
conform at all to these almost stereotypical expectations. The neighborhood did experience many urban
problems during and after transition, but they were
more the result of city and nationwide economic dis-
location which simultaneously occurred with the
influx of nonwhites. For example, Table 3 shows
that the median income for individuals in the
southwest sector of CPD 8 increased from twenty
percent in 1959 to twenty-five percent in 1969.
Maps 4 and 5 indicate that, except for a relatively
small number of apartment houses, in the early
1970s, the neighborhood had also not suffered
greatly from physical decay and economic decline.
This was true despite the fact that during the same
time outside the southwest sector of CPD 8 there was
considerable urban blight and significant numbers of
welfare cases.

     While most Central Brooklyn commercial
streets were almost devastated by the 1970s, the
main commercial avenue serving the Prospect-Lefferts-
Gardens neighborhood, Flatbush Avenue, was found to
be "sound" by a Housing and Urban Development study
in 1972. Commercial sectors outside the neighborhood
were found to be in need of extensive governmental
assistance because of the bleak business pictures
presented there. The general findings of the HUD
report in reference to the Prospect-Lefferts-
Gardens area were as follows:

          The section of Crown Heights with the
          highest income, smallest poverty popula-
          tion, and the highest proportion of owner-
          occupied and well-maintained buildings. . . .
          The Southwest corner has the highest

Table 3. FAMILY INCOME IN PROSPECT-
LEFFERTS-GARDENS 1959 AND 1969.

1959

Annual Income	Number	Percent
Total Families	7,369	100.0
Under $5,000	2,148	29.2
$5,000-$9,999	3,628	49.2
$10,000-$14,999	1,078	14.6
Over $15,000	514	7.0

1969

Annual Income (in 1959 Dollars)		
Total Families	6,833	100.0
Under $5,000	1,895	27.7
$5,000-$9,999	2,782	40.7
$10,000-$14,999	1,224	18.0
Over $15,000	931	13.6

Source: U.S. Census of Population, 1960 and 1970.

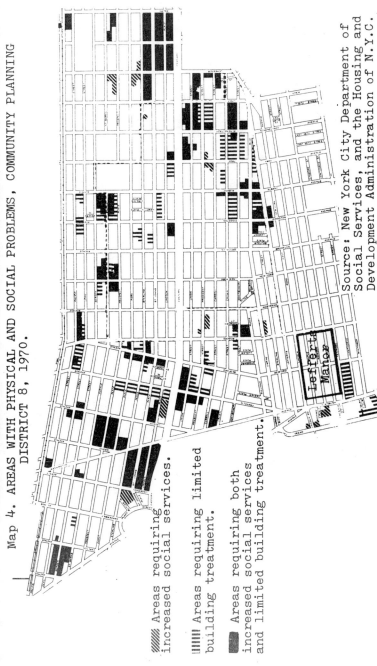

Map 4. AREAS WITH PHYSICAL AND SOCIAL PROBLEMS, COMMUNITY PLANNING DISTRICT 8, 1970.

Areas requiring increased social services.

Areas requiring limited building treatment.

Areas requiring both increased social services and limited building treatment.

Source: New York City Department of Social Services, and the Housing and Development Administration of N.Y.C.

From CHAMP Strategy, 1972: 19.

45

Map 5. WELFARE CASES* IN COMMUNITY PLANNING DISTRICT 8, 1971.

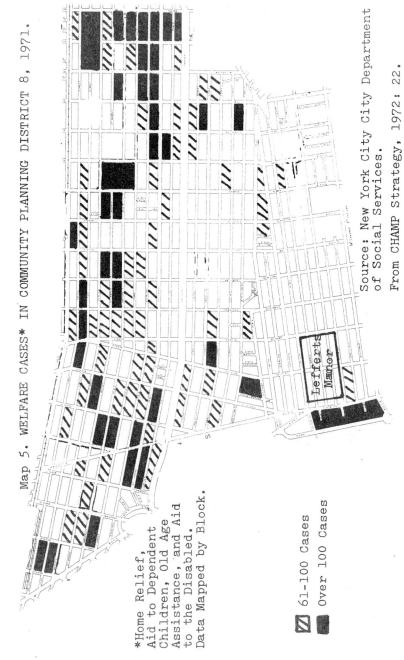

*Home Relief,
Aid to Dependent
Children, Old Age
Assistance, and Aid
to the Disabled.
Data Mapped by Block.

Source: New York City City Department
of Social Services.

From CHAMP Strategy, 1972: 22.

61-100 Cases

Over 100 Cases

46

percentage of middle-income families and
some of the finest housing in Crown Heights.
    The southwest corner includes the fine
Prospect-Lefferts-Gardens neighborhood where
half the families earn over $10,000 a year
while only 7 percent of the households receive welfare. (The Community Planning
District average is 19 percent.) A section
of the southwest has applied for designation as an Historical District by the City
Landmarks Preservation Committee.[8]

By 1978 the commercial streets which traverse the
neighborhood lost much of their vitality, but were
still, relative to other Central Brooklyn communities, attractive to large numbers of shoppers. My
own survey of the stores on the western edge of
Prospect-Lefferts-Gardens showed that while almost
half of the stores went out of business between
1973 and 1978, most were replaced by new, mainly
minority, businesses. Essentially, the ethnic
changes in the residential parts of the community
have been mirrored on the commercial strips. The
1977 summer "Blackout" riots in Brooklyn also
differentially affected certain parts of the Borough.
For example, Flatbush Avenue, which runs by
Prospect-Lefferts-Gardens, suffered a great deal of
looting but it was well outside of the neighborhood,
to the South where more severe social and physical
decline had already bypassed the neighborhood.

    Physical decline of a city neighborhood is
usually associated with major increases in local
crime rates. Prospect-Lefferts-Gardens is part of
the 71st Police Precinct in Brooklyn, which was
until the early 1970s a "moderate" per capita crime
precinct as demonstrated in Map 6. Although such a
designation was not much for community people to
cheer about, in comparison to nearby neighborhoods
they had much for which to be grateful. Local
groups have for over ten years been increasingly
concerned with what they see as an alarming
increase in area crime rates. Officials of the
precinct are quick to explain, however, that the
crime problem in the neighborhood was actuarially
low, and for this reason the neighborhood was in
many ways under-patrolled. In 1980 the 71st
Precinct had the second highest incidence of
reported crime in the city.

Map 6. PER CAPITA CRIME RATES BY PRECINCT, 1971

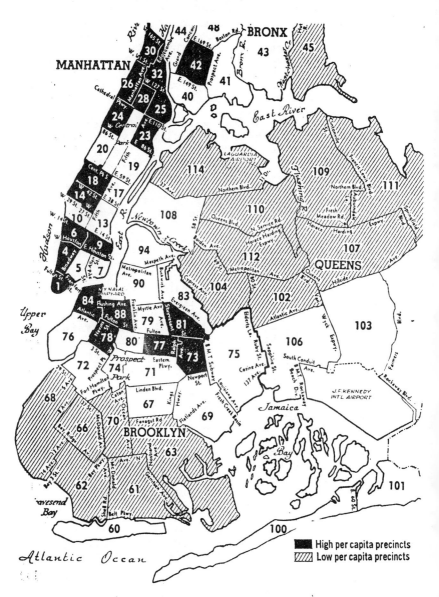

From <u>The New York Times</u>, February 14, 1972

Hot spots of local street crime are generally found on the extreme edges of the neighborhood where most of the low-income population lives and which spills into the rest of the community. Particularly dangerous pedestrian routes are near subway stations, and walking on commercial streets at night and in the early evening, as in most parts of New York City, is not advisable. As noted there still remains in the neighborhood a number of elderly people living in large apartment houses. They are especially concerned with the crime problem, as they are the most likely victims. Juvenile delinquency has also increased locally as a larger proportion of the total community population are youthful, poor and unemployed in summer months.

In general, the fear of crime in the neighborhood is always greater than the amount of crime itself. Symbolically, such perceptions of crime-filled streets can undermine the stability of any inner-city neighborhood and are therefore constant threats to the Prospect-Lefferts-Gardens area. Many of the elderly residents with whom I have spoken are so fearful of being attacked that some do not venture outside their apartments and have all their necessities delivered to them. Others go out only during the daytime and in the company of other elderly friends. One of my neighborhood elderly informants was mugged only a few weeks after his wife had her pocketbook snatched by a teenager. What might seem incredible to the reader is that people will remain in a community despite its problems. For example, in the spring of 1981, street crime became such a large problem that community members formed a security association and paid $200 per year for a private security patrol. To understand this it is necessary to understand the balance, or imbalance, of the positive and negative definitions residents hold of their community, and to realize how much, or how little, local residents have at stake in their homes, both economically and psychologically.

The question as to why the anticipated destruction of the Prospect-Lefferts-Gardens community has not yet occurred should be of great interest to the urban sociologist, and those who are generally interested in the urban scene. Although it is undeniable that larger scale social and economic forces played important parts in creating this anomaly, my research suggests that a special positive meaning connected to this particular neighborhood by many residents was the most important factor in its survival, and also the deflection of extensive urban blight from the area. If we are concerned with preventing urban decay, or rehabilitating those areas that have already undergone severe deterioration, symbolic values and definitions of residential places must be studied and understood by urban policy makers and implementers. Decisions about saving and improving urban communities should be based on an awareness by experts of the subjective, as well as the objective conditions, of neighborhood life. Community development plans, for example, might include public relations campaigns, such as those associated with suburban development, coordinated with physical reconstruction, demolition and rehabilitation in order to attract and keep desirable community members.

The study of the social and psychological processes set into motion by the movement of succeeding waves of ethnic and social class groups into Prospect-Lefferts-Gardens, and other Central Brooklyn neighborhoods, is reinforced by demogrphic, geographic, ecological and historical materials I have collected covering four centuries. Other materials employed are: oral histories from long time residents, personal documents such as letters provided by local informants, local and city-wide newspaper articles, intensive interviews of community leaders, and extensive participant-observation of formal and informal social groups in the community. A great deal of information was gathered merely by talking to people, and listening to people talk, at local information centers such as coffee shops, grocery stores and private gatherings. Personal contacts with informants at local police precincts, fire department, schools, sanitation and other public service locations also provided a great deal of information and, in particular, gave insight of public employees toward the Prospect-Lefferts-Gardens area. These attitudes have great influence on the kinds of city services provided to a local community.

The research immediately uncovered distinctive physical and social patterning in the neighborhood. The overall residential layout of the area, especially in reference to social class and ethnic segregation, was found to have changed very little over the entire lifespan of the area as a populated neighborhood--about eighty years. This has been accomplished, in part, by the repeated official sanction of locally produced land-use patterns via zoning regulations, traffic routing systems and restrictive covenants which have protected "special" parts of the community.

Although Prospect-Lefferts-Gardens has a long and significant "official" history, i.e., that found in history books, as a populated urban place it has had a relatively short existence. Often scholars studying modern urban communities forget that these neighborhoods, filled with buildings and people, had previously existed as woodlands, farms, rural areas, suburbs or as small towns. They may also not realize that events a century or more in the past continue to have influence on modern urban life. The most important factors in the rise and fall of some present-day urban areas may have taken place in the nineteenth, or even earlier, century when many urban neighborhoods were initially established or designed.

The nonwhite invasion of Prospect-Lefferts-Gardens is indeed dramatic, but it is only one part of a long series of invasions that have taken place over the entire lifespan of the community. Even the current in-migration of nonwhites contains a number of smaller ethnic "mini-invasions" that are not easily detected. The racial terms "black" and nonwhite obscure the fact that a large number of different non-European groups have moved into the area in significant numbers commencing around 1940. American blacks from southern rural areas and cities are mixed in with migrants from other northern cities and other New York City neighborhoods. Other black invaders began their migration to PLG in the Carribean, Central and South America, as well as England and Canada. In this group Haitians, Jamaicans, Barbadians, and Dominicans have been the major nationality components. Beginning in 1970 a large number of Asians and Middle Eastern peoples have also become visible in the area. Most of these families, Asian and Middle Eastern, live in apartments above stores on commercial streets while other foreign-born nonwhites form small ethnic pockets in various parts of the community. There is also a small Hispanic "barrio" in the center of Prospect-Lefferts-Gardens, as an example of the non-European community enclaves.

It is important to note that the Asian and Middle Eastern invasion of the neighborhood is related to the replacement of Jewish and other white-owned businesses in the area by recent immigrants, which gives the commercial strips an extremely diverse ethnic make-up. The drastic changes in the United States Immigration Law made in 1965 have made these more recent and exotic ethnic invasions possible. Earlier laws had especially discriminated against Asian, African, Middle Eastern and Western Hemisphere emigrants, and when quotas were raised they were quickly filled.

Prospect-Lefferts-Gardens has been the goal of selective invaders for almost one hundred years. In many ways the migration history of the community reflects the immigration history of the nation. In small neighborhoods, at the micro-social level, one can observe the processes of immigration, assimilation, urbanization and cultural accommodation up close. Just as the founders of European colonies in the New World set the tone for mainstream American society and culture, so did the original settlers, and their heirs set the standards for the future Prospect-Lefferts-Gardens community.

The key to understanding the situation in the wider neighborhood has been, and continues to be, knowing what takes place in the strategic Lefferts Manor, a small socially and economically select area within Prospects-Lefferts-Gardens where local elites have lived since the seventeenth century. Map 7 shows the location of the Manor and local environs. Most studies of residential succession have taken somewhat of an actuarial approach, but changes in a community and its character are not just functions of numbers. It is important for us to be able to appreciate the personal and group experiences of invaders as they come into contact with dominants and each other. We should also be made aware of the obvious and more subtle modifications in the local culture of community that results from these interactions. Most dramatically, three hundred years after the Dutch settled in the area, descendants of slaves, who may have worked this very soil, now walk upon

Map 7. LEFFERTS MANOR STREETS

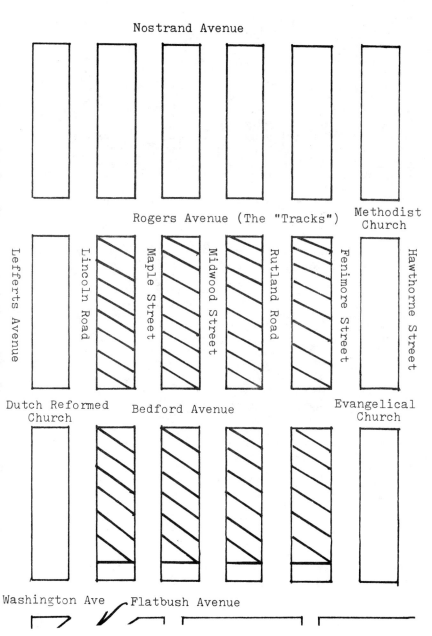

53

their own property as doctors, lawyers and school
teachers.

The symbolic aspect of residential succession
is an important and intriguing phenomenon, for it
brings into focus the historical imagery of a neighborhood and gives insight into the continuing
problems of community development and maintenance.
People who maintain their community must believe
that it is worth preserving and this belief is
always difficult to hold given the disenchantment
and alienation of modern urban society. Believing
that one's community is, so to speak, "sacred" in
the same sense that Romulus believed Roman soil to
be, also leads people on occasion to display the
less noble side of human nature. Objectively,
social scientists might not approve of it, but
protecting a community against the invasion of
minority groups, for example, can be viewed as a
"natural" feature of neighborhood stability.

The collection of groups who have over the
years inhabited and protected the Lefferts Manor
has been, aside from social class, extremely diverse.
All those who are identifiable as members of a multi-
tude of minority ethnic or religious groups (non-
WASPs) have had similar initial experiences in the
Manor as they sought to take their place as co-equals
with resident elites. When they first moved in,
hostility was directed toward them by the older more
established residents. This social rejection was
followed by the newcomers gradual acceptance into
the community, and their becoming part of the
dominant residential (not ethnic) group. Later,
as they became dominants they either directly or
indirectly participated in efforts to keep out
"undesirable" newcomers. Also, with each subsequent
invasion it was evident that the longest established
Manorites were the most likely to leave the
community. Those that chose to remain took it upon
themselves to informally and formally re-socialize
invaders or to make the most of a less than perfect
social situation. The excerpts from the Lefferts
Manor community newsletter, which was published on
and off for about twenty years, provides some of the
flavor of this local community socialization process.
They were taken from the Letters to the Editor
section of the Manor Echo.

Dear Editor,

In the spring and summer I enjoy walking
to the subway station by way of Maple
Street. The gardens are beautiful and the
grass is green. However, now that winter
snow and ice abound, I try to avoid Maple
Street. . . . Although many of the residents
are diligent about shoveling their sidewalks, there are a few constant delinquents
on the block who cause hazardous conditions
by not clearing their sidewalks properly.

                    Old Time Resident
                    January 1969

Dear Mr. Leffman,

I have lived on Midwood Street for many
years and always appreciated the quiet
atmosphere on the block. However, in
recent months we have been plagued by a
great deal of noise and boisterous laughter
in one of the homes on the block. What
course should I follow to stop this
nuisance?

                    Concerned
                    January 1969

Dear Mr. Leffman,

I sweep my sidewalks regularly and take the
garbage cans in when the sanitation trucks
have passed as most of my neighbors do.
However, there are a few people on the block
who leave them out for a good part of the
day.

                    Neat and Clean
                    January 1969

Dear Lefferts Manor Association,

Several people in the neighborhood put their
dogs in the backyard at 7:00 in the morning
and leave them there for at least an hour or
two. I work late and find that the noise of
all the dogs barking and howling at each
other interrupts my sleep.

                    Dog-tired
                    November 1974

Other articles in the Manor Echo mirror the
conversations of neighbors concerning unruly children,
unkept gardens, unswept sidewalks and uncurbed dogs.
It is these almost oblique networks of communication
within the Lefferts Manor community, which include
community meetings and the passing of unsigned notes
to troublesome neighbors or anonymous phone calls by
"concerned" residents, that have carried the Manor
"message" for about 70 years.

When speaking to Manorites about the history
of their community, during their own lifetimes, one
must remember that they are quite likely residues
of earlier dominant neighborhood groups. They tend
to evaluate changes in the Common in relation to
their own personal, and their reference groups'
ideals about the neighborhood at present, and what
is most often referred to as "better" times past.
To older Manor residents the community can never
again be the exclusive community it once was.

It is imperative to keep in mind that "history"
is merely a collection of stories told by different
people, and that everyone does not tell the same
story in the same way. The bulk of the following
sections on the Lefferts Manor are based on an
assemblage of various official and symbolic
histories. Some are personal accounts of the
history of the area provided by oldtimers and
newcomers. In every case, the stories which are
told, official or not, should not be regarded as
true or false, accurate or inaccurate, but as meaningful accounts that are used by people to explain
their own social worlds to themselves and others.

All histories are intended to create a desired
picture and to convey selective information and
meanings. In fact the "official" history of the
community was for the most gathered from documents
published and re-published by local community groups
to promote interest and pride in the neighborhood
and more recently to justify the demand for a special
Historical Landmark designation to help preserve the
character of the area, which was granted in the
autumn of 1979. Much of the material was provided
by people who learned that I was "writing a book"
about the community. One of these contributions
which was most useful for demonstrating the symbolic
value of local history, was a series of six booklets
reporting on the history of the "Original Six
Towns" of what is now the Borough of Brooklyn,

New York. The documents were published by the defunct borough newspaper, the Brooklyn Eagle, in 1946. The reason for the publication and distribution of these short history texts demonstrates clearly what is meant by an "intentional" history. According to Frank D. Schroth, the publisher of the Eagle:

> The borough is a community of homes, churches and schools, and in population is exceeded by only one city in the country. In importance it is second to none. It is the hope of the Brooklyn Eagle that the printing of these histories of the original settlements will interest not only our adult readers but--and this is more important--will also serve to make the youth of the Borough more conscious of the stirring events that have transpired in the last 300 years on the very ground they pass each day about their appointed tasks. . . . Each of the six towns has its own history, is great in its own right, and has characteristics which definitely contribute to the fascinating whole that is modern Brooklyn. The Eagle has attempted to "take Brooklyn apart" to show what makes it the fabulous place that is--the best known community in the world.[9]

Because of the propagandistic bent of history, one should not pay as much attention to details of "assumed" facts, as to how the interpretation of those facts has affected the current status of the Lefferts Manor and Prospect-Lefferts-Gardens. Not only have actual historical events and decisions by powerful people had an impact on the contemporary structure and function of the neighborhood, but also historically, the images of the community held by insiders and outsiders have had great impact on the local area.

Additionally, important aspects of history are often overshadowed by the attention to strict empirical realities. As a result, one often misses the moral texture and context of history. For example, an attempt has been made, where applicable, to find the similarities of experiences in the Lefferts Manor by different invading groups. It is especially interesting to hear the cries of outrage

by representatives of one ethnic group at being
defined by oldtimers as undesirable, and to see that
group make the next newcomers run the same social
gauntlet that they once had to run in order to be
accepted. The fact that "history repeats itself"
is a moral as well as an academic maxim.

The Social Character of the Manor

The Lefferts Manor could be any middle-class
urban neighborhood that was established in the late
nineteenth century. Here row upon row of sturdy,
well-kept, single-family homes are occupied by households headed by professional and semi-professional
men and women. In contrast to the turn-of-the-
century, many of the Manor's families are co-headed
by women who have returned to work after their
traditional roles of child rearing and housekeeping
became less important. The two-income family is an
increasingly common situation in middle-class urban
neighborhoods. Children grow up and move away.
Modern appliances reduce household chores to a
minimum with a concommitant decrease in the need
for full-time servants, who had always been an
integral part of "respectable" middle-class households in the past. Today, custom and prosperity
allow for the periodic "heavy" chores to be performed by contracted housekeepers or service
organizations. Traditionally, this work of washing
floors, windows and cleaning rugs had been overseen
by the "lady of the house." In the middle-class of
the Manor, the lady of the house is more and more
likely to be employed outside the home.

People who live in upper-middle-class neighborhoods seem to have limited sense of local community.
The social and geographic parameters of what
they would call their own neighborhood are small.
Upper-middle-class people tend to be oriented toward
their own property and their own homes. They live
inside their houses, and not as the less affluent,
outside of them. Ordinarily, they have relatively
few close friends who live with them in their
local neighborhood communities. A functional
explanation for this situation is that they have no
economic or social need for large numbers of more
intimate neighbors as compared to people in working-
class areas. The common place "neighboring"
activities which are features of urban neighborhood

living as cited by Suzanne Keller are infrequently
engaged in by most Manorites.[10] Whereas in most
lower-middle-class communities neighboring seems to
be a major source of social interaction, in the Manor
these activities are exceptions to the general rule
of simple, polite helloes and rare full-length conversations on the street, what Georg Simmel would
have called "meaningless sociability."[11] Seldom are
neighbors invited inside for coffee, tea, an afternoon or evening drink and a "chat." People in the
Lefferts Manor normally do not know each other very
well at all; they are merely familiar to each other.
In this regard, Manorites are exceptionally good
examples of Louis Wirth's "urban life style."[12]

A major exception to the rule of "mere
familiarity" in the Lefferts Manor are the social
groups that form which are composed of small numbers
of women with pre-school age children who come
together symbiotically. Mothers get together to
allow their restless children opportunities to play
with others, but as the children grow older they are
usually sent to a wide range of nursery and kinder-
garten programs that are determined by the relative
wealth of parents, and their ethnic and religious
backgrounds. Local public or parochial schools
might provide an opportunity to continue these
early bonds, but most Manorites do not send their
children to local educational institutions, unless
the schools are as "exceptional" and prestigious as
the parents believe themselves to be.

Usually, the fathers of Manor children are
only peripherally involved in the female "near
groups" that are child-oriented. They are more
likely to be the topics of conversation in these
groups than participants in them. Most fathers also
do not concern themselves to any great degree with
the task of childrearing. In some ways this child-
oriented aspect of the Manor is similar to the
suburban communities studied by James S. Coleman.[13]
Different from the suburbs, however, is the fact
that single cohorts of children are never a major
proportion of the Lefferts Manor population. In
more advantaged families in the Manor the mother
as well as the father retreats from extensive
interaction with children. The children are "taken"
care of by nurses, sitters, tutors, schools, after-
care, day camps, sleep-away camps and other, often
expensive services, which leave parents free to

pursue their own interests.

People who live in the Lefferts Manor do not
become overly upset or feel great loss when a
neighbor passes away. Neither the sight of moving
vans nor funeral cars generate much community sadness,
except in the limited, singly affected household,
and perhaps a close neighbor. The major concern
when the Manor loses a member is focused upon who
will replace the departed. Manorites want to be
sure that the "right" kind of family moves into the
vacated space, a family that is their equal.

Few middle-aged Manorites have such great
personal emotional stakes and attachments to the
community that they could not be torn away, particularly if the move is associated with greater economic
and social advancement. It is the older community
members and the youngest homeowners who have the
greatest psychic investments in their particular
homes and the Manor itself. The elderly are emo-
tionally welded to the neighborhood because such
a large portion of their lives is connected to
their present address. Their homes are their own
personal historical museums. The younger residents
are firmly attached to the Manor due to the newness
of their experience as homeowner, and the immediacy
of their personal investment in their property. The
thrill of owning your first home tends to wear off
slowly, and after five or six years is completely
gone. Re-decorating and maintenance becomes a
chore and people start debating the cost of re-
investment, and weighing the relative value of
improving their property. This is a crucial stage,
for those who decide to re-invest in their property,
and the Manor, generally stay on forever. The
decision to stay, or to move, is based on the
relative weight of positive and negative definitions
homeowners have of the Lefferts Manor, as compared
to other housing opportunities.

Manorites are woven together by intricate and
vague networks of communication. Several opinion
and information leaders are located on each block.
Most often the source of news about the community
is either a non-working older woman, or an active
young woman with small children. Both of these
kinds of Manorites are most likely to be aware of
what is going on locally. They also have the
greatest opportunity to collect and distribute

60

news and tid-bits of gossip, about neighbors and the neighborhood. There are also a few community activists in the Manor and local community organizations which distribute flyers and hold meetings, but most residents have neither the time nor the inclination for community involvement.

Although few Manorites come into direct contact with opinion and information leaders, the disseminators are indirectly linked to almost the whole population of the community through intermediaries. Contact with, and information about, geographically near co-residents of the Lefferts Manor is slight, and the degree of contact and knowledge even further as distances between households increase. Manorites who live around the corner from each other are virtual strangers to each other in most cases.

When Manorites walk in their neighborhood they usually take the most direct path; to a subway or bus stop, retail store, the park, and then proceed directly home. They take account of very little during these trips through these "psychological tunnels" which take them outside of the Manor itself. Only the most outstanding and obvious features of the physical environment are noticed; an abandoned store, a fire-damaged building, police cars with flashing lights, or an ambulance parked in the Common might catch their eye. Even these events merit only minor attention and little comment. Since the recent decay began outside of the boundaries of the Lefferts Manor, they venture less frequently outside their enclave by foot. We might wish to argue that the Commoners have little "collective consciousness" as community members, but they certainly have a "collective unconsciousness." Jane Jacobs had noted in Death and Life of Great American Cities that long straight blocks, such as those that traverse the Lefferts Manor, tend to reduce perceptual awareness of the physical environment (1961).

Although the life styles and behavioral traits of Manorites are by and large similar to those displayed by other middle-class urbanites, the Lefferts Manor is also unique. Uniqueness is, however, a universal attribute of neighborhoods. Ordinary people always talk about their communities, and themselves, as though there were no others exactly like them. Even the ways that Manorites define the special attributes of their community are similar to

61

the ways that others define their neighborhoods.
The general elements of unique description which
emerge when one asks a person to describe their
neighborhood are: firstly, a name, then some kind
of geographic coordinates, e.g., relationships to a
larger geographic area such as the city as a whole,
benchmarks or local landmarks, kinds and styles of
housing, and the kinds of people who now live or
have lived in the neighborhood. All these data make
it possible to set the community apart, symbolically,
from the rest of the world. When I began interviewing people in the Manor in 1969, many people noted
in their description that it was "white." Then it
became "integrated." Today it is increasingly being
defined as "black." The importance of the racial
aspect of community definition in the Manor, however,
has never been as emphatic as that expressed by
whites who live in working-class communities in
Brooklyn. To them neighborhoods are either "white"
or "black" (good and bad, respectively) and integrated
neighborhoods are incomprehensible.

It should also be emphasized that Manorites,
as compared to working class people, place racial
identity nearer the end of their description of
community. Ask someone where they live and they will
tell you in a patterned way about the "special" qualities of their neighborhood. Being special is then a
necessary component of community definition. In
order to identify one's community, unique qualities
and characteristics are needed, and if not readily
available they will be sought out or created on the
spot. Similarly, individual human beings are prone
to think of themselves as being "different" from
others despite the sociological argument which can
be made against this assumption of particularity.

In the modern urban world it is extremely
difficult to distinguish unique people from the
collection of mass-produced people, and personalities, we encounter in everyday life. Perhaps as a
response to living among this amorphous mass of
bodies, each of the individuals and individual types
of people we meet seems to have some unusual "line"
or story, but if one listens carefully the "lines"
we are given all sound the same. In order to be
our selves and not someone else, we must prove to
others that we are peculiar in some way. Names,
addresses, occupations, heights, weights and
biographies are the things we provide to audiences

to demonstrate who we are, as opposed to some other person.

An important aspect of self-definition is the place in which a person lives. As stated by A.E. Parr:

> Other things permitting, the individual will choose his surroundings according to the preferences and demands of his own personality. When he exercises his choice there will unavoidably be feedback from his selection to the psychological mechanisms that made it. This implies a two-way relationship between mind and milieu in which the environment might well prove to be the determinant, as well as a product of attitudes and personality. (1970:16)

Even when one's home is not a result of personal choice, but a product of coercion, it still has a great effect on personal identity. A man in prison is not so much a "criminal" as he is a "convict" or "inmate."[14] People who are convicted criminals but who have avoided confinement neither are called "cons" or "ex-cons," nor do they suffer the same degradation, or carry the same stigma, as one who has gone to prison. This is only one example of the power of residence to influence and determine socially meaningful definitions of people in society. Similarly, Louis Wirth and Kenneth B. Clark have demonstrated the negative aspects of ghetto living on the personal and group identities of their inhabitants.[15]

On the other extreme of meaningful residence are the values ascribed to high class areas and addresses. In John L. Hess's New York Times article, "Snobbery about One's Address Remains Alive in the City," it was noted that particularly the newly rich are willing to spend considerable sums of money for rent in buildings which have a "name," or in which prominent people live. For example, when selling apartments in the United Nations Plaza building, a luxury high-rise on Manhattan's East Side, prospective buyers were seduced to "Come and Join Truman Capote and Bobby Kennedy."[16]

Manorites, as dissociated from each other as they are, still share a common identity as residents

of a specific place. They have a common identity
even though many may not realize it. The ways by
which environments, or more specifically, neighborhood communities, are defined are similar to the
ways that social selves are created. Furthermore,
the social and psychological definitions of place
and self interact with one another and are mutually
affected by many common causes. The history of the
Lefferts Manor and the biographies of its members
are inexorably intertwined.

Chapter III

WOODLAND TO CITY NEIGHBORHOOD:

300 YEARS OF CHANGE

The official history of the Lefferts Manor, and surrounding areas, begins with the colonization and development of Brooklyn by the Dutch settlers over three hundred years ago. In 1661 a large parcel of woodland was deeded to Cornelius Janse by Peter Stuyvesant, Governor of New Amsterdam on behalf of the West Indian Company, Netherlands Charter. Map 8 is a reproduction of a seventeenth-century map of Brooklyn. Today, the Lefferts Manor, Prospect-Lefferts-Gardens, Crown Heights, East New York, Brownsville and parts of Bedford-Stuyvesant, Flatbush and Bushwick have replaced the thick woods, running streams, ponds and marshes. The deer and other abundant wild life of pre-colonial Brooklyn have been replaced by stray cats, dogs, and descendants of Norwegian rats.

Cornelius Janse was the first of what was later to be called the "Lefferts family" to settle in the Americas. The Lefferts family eventually became prominent in town, city and state-wide political affairs. The land deeded to Janse was acquired by the Dutch West Indian Company in typical Peter Minuet fashion. The Canarsie Indians, who inhabited the territory, gave it over to the Dutch for one hundred guilders in "sewant" (mostly sea shells), four blankets, pistols, a few rounds of gunpowder, one and a half barrels of strong beer and three cans of brandy.

Dutch control of New Amsterdam and the surrounding area did not last very long. In 1664 English rule came to the Dutch colony. Due, however, to the terrible mismanagement of the Duke of York, who oversaw the English colony, "New York" experienced a number of fiscal and political crises which caused the citizenry to revolt. In 1673 the city was recaptured by the Dutch. They evidently did not intend to keep the territory for they voluntarily returned it to the British the next year after only a slight show of force. The continued inefficiency

Map 8. BROOKLYN, 1634

Flatbush, which appears to have been settled about 1634, is one of the most historic towns in all America. Its boundaries, indicated by the solid black lines on the map above, are described on page 5.

New Lots, which includes Brownsville and East New York, was once part of the orginal town of Flatbush. New Lots became a separate town in its own right in 1852.

From Historic and Beautiful Brooklyn,

Brooklyn Eagle, 1947.

of local English officials led the British Governor,
Thomas Dongan, to call a Representative Assembly in
1683 to try to straighten out the city's problems
and those of nearby towns. One of these problems
was a dispute between the towns of Brooklyn and
Flatbush over their respective boundaries. The
argument was finally settled after intense negotia-
tions in 1685 with the setting of their common town
borders at the northern edge of the Lefferts (Janse)
family property. This placed the Lefferts estate in
the town of Flatbush. Map 9 shows the boundaries of
the estate in relation to the present-day Lefferts
Manor.

An oak tree on the northern limit of the
Lefferts estate served as the benchmark for separating
the municipalities. The tree, called "Dongan Oak,"
stood just off Flatbush Road, which was the major
route connecting the two towns. The original Lefferts
family homestead building stands near the Dongan Oak
and serves today as a museum-landmark in Prospect
Park. The site is about a quarter-mile north of
the Lefferts Manor. The house was first located
near the center of the Manor, but was moved to the
park location shortly after the major urban development of the area took place.

During the eighteenth century John Lefferts,
the family patriarch, was very active in the political
and social life of Flatbush, as were the members of
the Vanderbilt, Cortelyou and other power clans who
had estates near the present-day Manor. John
Lefferts, for example, served as a member of the
American Provisional Congress. During the Revolutionary War the Crown Heights and Prospect-Lefferts-
Gardens area was the site of many important skirmishes
and strategic troop movements in the wide-ranging
"Battle of Long Island" (sometimes referred to as
the Battle of Brooklyn). Map 10 shows the Battle
in relation to Crown Heights today. One of the most
fateful encounters between Revolutionary and British
troops took place near the Manor:

> It was in the vicinity of the northerly
> edge of the Lefferts farm that the historic
> revolutionary battle of Brooklyn Heights
> took place, markers of which appear at
> various points in Prospect Park. It was a
> disastrous day for the Americans, many
> prisoners being taken, among them Generals

Map 9. THE OLD LEFFERTS FARM

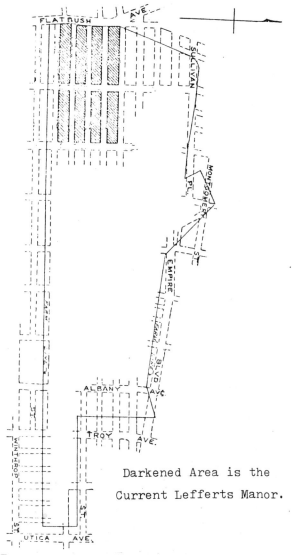

Darkened Area is the
Current Lefferts Manor.

From <u>Lefferts Manor Association</u> Brochure,
March, 1938: 13.

Map 10. CROWN HEIGHTS DURING THE AMERICAN REVOLUTION

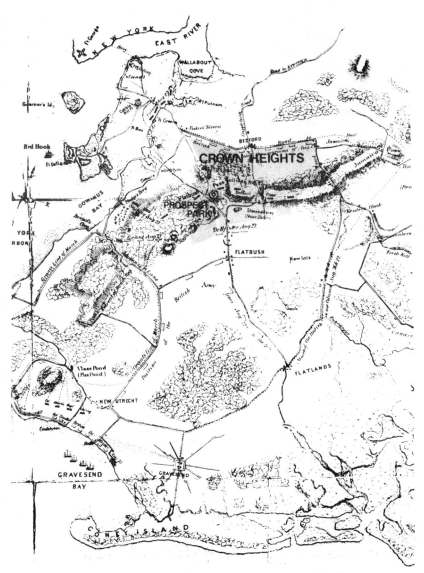

Map of the Battle of Brooklyn-August 27, 1776.
From <u>A HISTORY OF BROOKLYN</u> by Henry R. Stiles, 1867.

Sullivan, Sterling and Woodhull. After an
orderly retreat, General Washington took
his army to Harlem.

It was in this battle that Alexander
Hamilton entered the American Army as Captain
of Artillery and while actively engaged here-
abouts Hamilton was thrown into contact with
the Commander-in-Chief for the first time and
his superior abilities were brought to
General Washington's attention. This was
the beginning of that great friendship which
continued between these remarkable men during
the dark days of defeat as well as the
brighter ones of triumph and splendor which
came later.[1]

During the extended Long Island campaign, the
northern slope of the present-day neighborhood served
as a "Crow's Nest" for Revolutionary Army spotters,
who were guarding the Bedford Pass at the juncture
of the towns of Brooklyn and Flatbush. Some histori-
ans attribute the current name of Crown Heights to
its role in this important battle. The British were
expected to attack at this pass in their northward
advance through Brooklyn. Therefore, General George
Washington's army heavily defended the pass. It
seemed logical that British forces would attempt to
defeat the American forces at this point as it was
nearest the two important roads, which provided the
shortest and easiest routes to the rest of Washington's
army.

The major confrontation between opposing forces,
however, did not take place as anticipated at the
Bedford Pass. The British outmaneuvered the Americans
and ran an end-run around the heavily defended positions. As a result the battle was lost and Washington's troops were forced to retreat.

Flatbush Road now exists as Flatbush Avenue, a
major commercial street which still funnels traffic
from the south of Brooklyn toward "downtown"
businesses and industries, as well as to Manhattan.
The other road, Clove Road, has been for the most part
obliterated by the present grid street pattern. Its
skeletal remains are still visible to the careful eye
in the form of narrow parcels of city-owned property,
which traverse the back yards of homes located on the
eastern extreme of Prospect-Lefferts-Gardens. As is
true for most of New York City's historical relics,

very little remains standing which would indicate
the area's importance during Colonial and Revolutionary periods.

In 1788, Peter (son of John) Lefferts was sent
to the New York State Convention in Poughkeepsie as
a county delegate. The convention was called to adopt
the United States Constitution and Peter Lefferts was
later to become a New York State Senator. In 1821
Peter Lefferts was the sole Kings County delegate
(today the Borough of Brooklyn is coterminous with
the county of Kings), and Congressional Representative
to the New York State Convention at which the property
qualification for suffrage was removed.

The populations of the town of Flatbush and
the City of Brooklyn grew rapidly during the nineteenth century, but the Lefferts area remained
largely undeveloped and rural in appearance. The
luxurious mansions and broad estates of the Lefferts,
Vanderbilts and other notables were virtually the
only structures in the Lefferts Manor neighborhood
standing on either side of Flatbush Road. In 1860,
however, the City of Brooklyn began expanding at
an exponential rate, and its spreading web of streets
crept toward the semi-rural areas of Flatbush.
Although the Town of Flatbush was still a separate
municipality, it was included in planning maps for
City of Brooklyn development. This was typical of
the "imperialistic" acts of the City of Brooklyn,
which began in 1854 to absorb neighboring towns and
villages to meet the growing demand for commercial,
industrial and residential properties.[2] Flatbush
itself was not annexed into Brooklyn until 1894,
but the pre-annexation growth of Brooklyn had a
major impact on the eventual social and physical
character of the area. The boundaries and significant features of the Town of Flatbush in 1842 are
shown in Map 11.

The Lefferts Manor area was, in 1880, still
largely woodland and a few partially cleared farms
close by to a sprawling urban park, Prospect Park.
The section retained its suburban charm until relatively late for a number of reasons, not the least
of which was the fact that local elites continued to
maintain their estates in the area. Unfortunately,
shortly after 1880 these estates began to be subdivided and sold to developers. In place of the
sprawling grounds and palatial homes of the rich

71

Map 11. THE TOWN OF FLATBUSH, 1842.

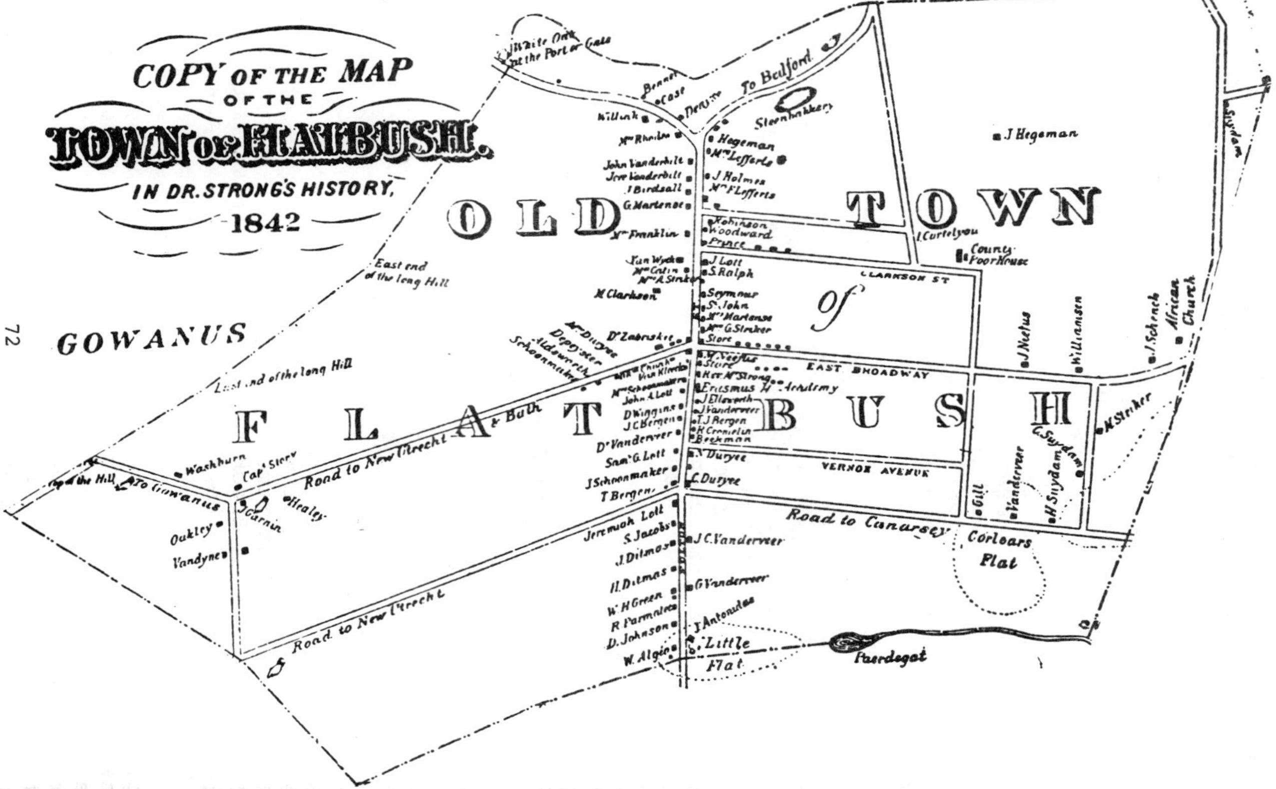

COPY OF THE MAP
OF THE
TOWN OF FLATBUSH,
IN DR. STRONG'S HISTORY.
1842

and powerful, a wide variety of single and multiple-
family dwellings were constructed. Flatbush Avenue
quickly became a busy commercial street with many
stores. The residential development of the area
picked up more steam in the first two decades of
the twentieth century, and continued until the 1950s
when construction of residential buildings ceased
completely. Virtually all of the housing built since
1890 still remains standing in the Prospect-Lefferts-
Gardens area. A few buildings have been replaced
over the years, primarily by higher-density apartment houses. In general, it is the single and two-
family homes which have best weathered the passing
of the years.

The Lefferts Manor and Prospect-Lefferts-Gardens
have benefitted greatly by an early experiment in
Garden City urban planning. In 1870, Eastern Parkway,
a wide tree-lined boulevard was constructed on the
northern ridge of Crown Heights to the north. It
was part of a comprehensive city plan for Brooklyn
designed by Calvert Vaux and Frederick Law Olmstead,
which included large urban parklands such as Prospect
Park. Magnificent thoroughfares were planned to
facilitate the development pattern of a "Garden
City." Although the plan was never fully implemented,
it captured the interest of the city's wealthy and
middle-class families. Exquisite mansions as well
as luxurious apartment houses eventually lined the
parkway, encircled the park and insured that Crown
Heights, Lefferts Manor and other strategic locations
in the borough would be protected from the ugly urban
sprawl that was to rapidly overcome less advantaged
neighborhoods. The parkway and related development
of plazas and cultural centers meant that Crown
Heights and the Lefferts Manor would become fashionable communities. It was not until the 1950s that
local homes and apartment houses, originally built
for the elites of Brooklyn society, were to fall
into the hands of the less affluent Brooklynites.

The Lefferts Manor has a long history as a
place, but a relatively short one as an urban
neighborhood. It began as a "potential" neighborhood
at the end of the nineteenth century when many of the
real estate holdings of "blue-blooded" Brooklyn
families were sold off and subdivided for industrial,
commercial and residential development. The Lefferts
family occupied a homestead estate and a larger
surrounding tract of land which included the Lefferts

73

Manor and most of Prospect-Lefferts-Gardens. The
estate had roughly the same boundaries as today's
Manor community. The fact that the site was the
original family patriarch's homestead convinced the
Lefferts heirs to sanctify the Manor section by
placing restrictions on the use of the land. A
covenant which "ran with the land" (into perpetuity)
was included in the deed for the property, then
largely vacant.

The covenant stipulated that the section be
built up as a respectable single-family community.
No commercial use of property was permitted; therefore there were to be no stores, rooming houses or
multiple-family dwellings, only substantial single-
family homes. In this way the Lefferts heirs sought
to preserve symbolic integrity of their ancestors in
much the same way as did the ancient Romans and
Greeks. The property was not, however, sanctified
by religious ceremony but by legal process.

Indians, Geology and Transportation

Although the impact of families such as the
Lefferts can be noticed on the maps of modern
Brooklyn in the form of street names and historical
landmarks, ordinary people's influences can only be
discovered through investigation. Before the
European, primarily Dutch settlement, others had lived
on this western tip of Long Island. Various Original
American tribes--like the Canarsie and Rockaway, who
are offshoots of the Delaware and Algonquin peoples--
had permanent and temporary homes here. They came
from many miles away, at different times of year, to
fish in the Hudson and East Rivers for salmon, or to
collect oysters, scallops, clams and other varieties
of the abundant sea life in and around New York Bay.
The modern lack of respect for the natural environment
has led to heavy pollution of New York waters and
seafood delicacies now must be brought to the city
from places many miles away.

Almost all of the Original American influence on
Brooklyn has been forgotten, but one can still make
tenuous connections between their habitation of the
area and modern urban problems. Part of the Prospect-
Lefferts-Gardens area covers what once was the
"Steenbakeray," or Stone Bakery Pond. Before Dutch
settlement of Brooklyn, local tribes believed that

74

the misty waters were inhabited by their spirts of
the dead. It was to them sacred waters. When the
Dutch took over they built the Bakery on the edge
of the waters, and during subsequent years the pond
and related marshlands were slowly drained and filled
by farmers, and finally built upon. During the
seventeenth century local farmers thought they had
seen sea serpents swimming in the water and one
reported seeing balls of fire hanging over the
mysterious pond.

These ancient spirits, of course, have no
influence today, but some mysterious occurrences are
reported in homes near where once the pond existed.
Houses that were built upon the drained and filled
area are prone to have many problems. Houses creak
and groan, windows move down and window shades roll
up suddenly. This is not due to resident polter-
geists, or Indian spirits, but the weight of the
heavy stone structures resting upon soft, spongy
substrata. The homes in that area continue to
float and settle on the semi-solid ground. When
the foundations slowly slip back and forth, strange
things are bound to happen.

Historical decisions such as these, to fill
and build upon marshland, have definite influences
on modern events. The effects include the damp,
wet and leaking cellar floors and occasional sewer
back-ups into basements because the local water
table is high and rises even higher after heavy
rainfalls. The streams that once ran into and out
of the pond also continue to plague the present-day
environment. There are no streams visible in
Prospect-Lefferts-Gardens today, as in the rest of
Brooklyn, but the streams are still there. Streams
continue to run, although more diffusely than before
urbanization, under the concrete and stone that was
laid over them. This causes the undermining of
sidewalks, streets and some house foundations. In
addition, other problems are caused by the ground
water that is simply forced through stone and brick
walls into basements by stream-generated pressure.
Topographically, the Prospect-Lefferts-Gardens
community slopes from the north toward the south,
so it is the northern basement walls that are the
wettest.

If one were to write a chronicle of the "Lost
Streams of Brooklyn," the records of the Department

of Highways would be a valuable archive. The
Department is called upon to repair damanged streets
after heavy rainfalls. The rain increases the volume
and velocity of the underground water, and the flow
washes away gravel and other supporting material
under pavement. The weight of traffic over the
space, then, depresses the roadway, creating a
clearly defined gully. An interview with an official
of the City Water Department confirmed these specu-
lations by noting that when the streets were hastily
constructed in this part of the city, road crews did
not provide conduits for existing streams but simply
dammed them by building across their path. Sewers
and storm drains were also not built in accordance
with natural stream paths.

    The streets and highways that were constructed
in Brooklyn were the result of high level decisions
that had important consequences for the Lefferts
Manor, and its environs. In particular, the laying
out of the grid patterns for future streets in
Brooklyn by city planners in 1835 were especially
important. The grid anticipated the annexation of
Flatbush and the real estate boom that was to
follow. Street grids tended to spread traffic and
to inhibit the concentration of industrial areas in
the middle of the borough. Flatbush became for the
most part a collection of primarily residential
communities, each with a somewhat distinct ethnic
and social class character.

    American city planners employed the grid
pattern because it allowed for rapid expansion as
urban population mushroomed. The cities grew so
fast in the nineteen hundreds that more aesthetically
pleasing formulas for urban design were not attempted.
This is part of the reason why so many New World
cities seem to be so similar in appearance, and why
it is so difficult to get lost, even in cities
where one has never been. The experience of living
in one American city helps us to orient ourselves in
another. The street numbering and lettering systems
are part of this uniform urban transportation
network.

    The grid pattern, however, does not merely have
physical results. There are social and psychological
consequences of this kind of urban growth plan.
Lewis Mumford states it this way:

The development of transporation caused
the traffic avenue to become the dominant
component in nineteenth-century design;
the emphasis changed from facilities for
settlement to facilities for movement.
By means of the traffic avenue, often
ruthlessly cutting through urban tissue
that once had been organically related to
neighborhood life, the city as a whole
became more united perhaps; but at the cost
of destroying, or at least seriously undermining, neighborhood life.   (1968:60-61)

Most of the "new" urban neighborhoods lost contact and continuity with the past. As they emerged
from the grid iron, communities had to find more
mechanical bases for solidarity, which were not
offered by the organically organized urban world.
They found that solidarity in homogeneous groupings
by social class, ethnicity, religion, race and
occupation. Only in a few exceptional circumstances
did accidents or designs allow older historical neighborhoods, forged by topography and historical events,
to survive intact. People found it harder to get lost
in the city and also more difficult to feel at home.
Neighborhoods and neighborhood residents had to create
their own uniqueness in order to stand out from
potentially anonymous communities. The urban
resident could more easily find himself on a map
than within some meaningful organic whole.
Aesthetically, the grid pattern, as noted by urban
planning critic Jane Jacobs, led to monotonous,
boring and generally unpleasing cityscapes.[3] The
uniform street system also bred uniform housing types
which resulted in row upon row of the exact same
house.

Besides the aesthetic pollution of Brooklyn's
once charming woodlands and farms, the comprehensive
transportation and development design facilitated
the rapid urbanization of the Lefferts Manor and
surrounding areas. Prospect-Lefferts-Gardens and
Flatbush in effect were not really "urban" until
the turn of the century. By 1930 they were completely citified, with high density housing and
bustling shopping areas. Many people today remark
at the rate of growth of suburbanization, and the
more recent urbanization of the suburbs. They would
not have been so surprised had they known that not
too long ago many of the nation's inner city slums

were also suburban communities.

Flatbush Avenue which runs north and south on the western edge of the Lefferts Manor led out of a fully developed City of Brooklyn in 1860, and cut through the rural and semi-rural countrysides, connecting small towns and villages together in a comprehensive urban and suburban web. It functioned then in the same way that parkways and expressways tie modern suburbs to the metropolis. It was on these major routes, in the nineteenth century, that commuter transportation lines were built, first exclusively as surface and later as underground lines as well. As early as 1860 a horse-drawn trolley car travelled back and forth between the Town of Flatbush and the bustling port and mercantile centers of the City of Brooklyn. The transit company was privately owned and run. In 1896 the line was electrified, heralding the beginning of twentieth-century mass transportation innovations.

In addition, during the late 1800s a steam railroad with "diminutive engine and open, cross seated passenger cars" ran by the Manor on the way from Atlantic Avenue to the popular oceanside resort of Brighton Beach. Atlantic Avenue was then an important east-wide corridor which led to the farm-lands of western Long Island. The world famous Coney Island amusement park was built in 1897 adjacent to Brighton Beach and forever changed the character of that once exclusive resort area. Today, Brighton Beach is referred to as a sort of "poor man's Miami Beach"; in 1980 over half of its residents were sixty years of age or older.

It was not until the extension of major subway lines into the greater Flatbush area that the suburban to urban metamorphosis took place. In 1904 the con-struction of the Brighton Line was started. Eight years later, excavations for the Nostrand Avenue line were also begun. The two routes straddled the Lefferts Manor and Prospect-Lefferts-Gardens. Spurred on by the availability of rapid transit to Manhattan, as well as downtown Brooklyn, when the lines were opened in 1920, a building and population explosion took place in Flatbush. The travel time to Manhattan, for example, was reduced by thirty minutes and put workers within easy commuting distance with their jobs.

North of Flatbush, in Crown Heights and Bedford-Stuyvesant, the great "transportation revolution" had taken place several years earlier, and they were already bursting at the seams with excess population. The rapid build-up to the south of these neighborhoods was not uniform and did not result in the uniform distribution of dense urban neighborhoods as was true of Bedford-Stuyvesant. Some upper-middle-class, one-family, suburban-like communities, such as the Lefferts Manor, were left as idyllic enclaves of privilege in a vast collection of more ordinary urban neighborhoods. The phenomenal growth of Brooklyn is demonstrated in Table 4 and Figure 1, which show that it grew from 1,166,582 residents in 1900 to 2,560,401 in 1930. In essence, every ten years a city for 500,000 residents had been built. These figures also chart the growth and racial changes in Brooklyn, Flatbush and Prospect-Lefferts-Gardens.

Rapid transit made economically feasible the construction of large-scale apartment houses of fifty units or more in Flatbush because subways connecting the area to downtown jobs made apartments marketable. The concentration of population in turn fostered the growth of retailing industries in the area. Population densities and types of housing available varied, but with a certain regularity: near subway stations density was high, and apartment houses dominated the scene; further away the densities decreased, and single-family homes were in the majority. The Lefferts Manor was close by to both the Brighton and Nostrand subway lines, but its covenant which restricted the use of property to one-family, noncommercial uses, protected it from apartment house developers, real estate speculators and eventual oblivion. Regrettably, the elite community was surrounded by large imposing apartment houses which forever blocked out its suburban horizons. The Manor became a canyon of low-rise houses almost encircled by steep five- and six-story building walls.

Protecting the Community: Covenant and Zoning

In 1893, the heirs to the Lefferts family estate divided their property into six hundred contiguous lots, fixing the area as a first class neighborhood

Table 4. POPULATION GROWTH, BROOKLYN AND PROSPECT-
LEFFERTS GARDENS, TOTAL AND BLACK, 1790-1980.

	Total Brooklyn	Black Brooklyn	Total Flatbush	Total P-L-G	Black P-L-G
1790	4,495		941		
1800	5,740		946		
1810	8,303		1,159		
1820	11,187		1,027		
1830	20,535		1,143		
1840	47,613		2,099		
1850	138,882		3.177		
1860	279,122		3,471		
1870	419,921		6,309		
1880	599,495				
1890	838,547				
1900	1,166,582	18,367		6,194	
1910	1,634,351	22,708		10,749	
1920	2,018,356	31,912		11,681	
1930	2,560,401	68,921		24,782	84
1940	2,698,285	107,263		27,142	125
1950	2,738,175	208,478		28,653	112
1960	2,627,319	371,405		25,272	2,474
1970	2,606,012	656,194		25,469	11,690
1980	2,230,936	722,316			

Sources: Ira Rosenwaike, Population History of New York City. Syracuse: Syracuse University Press, 1972; and the U.S. Census of Population, 1900, 1910, 1920, 1930, 1940, 1950, 1960, 1970, and 1980.

Figure 1. SELECTED POPULATION GROWTH FOR BROOKLYN,
FLATBUSH AND PROSPECT-LEFFERTS-GARDENS, 1790-1980.

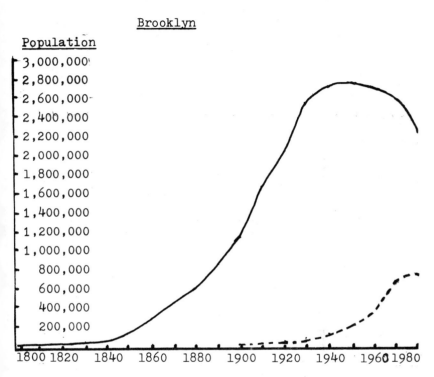

Brooklyn

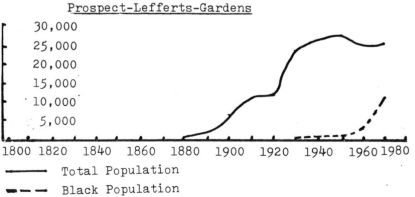

Prospect-Lefferts-Gardens

——— Total Population

━ ━ ━ Black Population

for private, single-family homes. The restrictive
covenant which was drawn established a moral and
legal code for present and future generations of
Manorites. Shortly afterwards, the Lefferts Manor
community faced the first cf a never-ending series
of attacks on its symbolic and territorial integrity.
In 1905, when the "building boom" began in Flatbush,
the Manor was only partially completed, and so there
was no organized protest against encroachment by
nearby businesses and apartment houses. By 1919,
however, the elite neighborhood of doctors, lawyers,
executives, businessmen and politicians formed the
Lefferts Manor Association "to help preserve and
maintain the high character of the neighborhood."
The following newspaper articles chronicle the
widely publicized efforts of the Association to
defeat its "enemies."[4]

> May 19, 1922 - LEFFERTS MANOR ASSOCIATION
> WINS
>
> Supreme Court Justice Lewis J. Fawcett
> made a judgement against Frederick C. Solz,
> owner of 39 Rutland Road "for violation of
> a covenant in the deed" which prohibited
> other than one-family use of the property.
> He had rented furnished rooms.

> May 15, 1926 - LEFFERTS MANOR COMMENDS POLICE
>
> At the annual meeting of the Lefferts
> Manor Association . . . the attorney for the
> Association reported that "action was pend-
> ing in Supreme Court" against the owner of
> 66 Maple Street for violation of the covenant.
> Other items were: tree spraying, and a
> request to the Police Commissioner to post
> signs at the entrance to the Manor restrict-
> ing traffic to "pleasure vehicles" and
> lightweight business vehicles.

> January 18, 1928 - LEFFERTS MANOR PROTESTS
> SCHOOL
>
> . . . the community protested against the
> building of a Public School on the border of
> the Manor. They appealed to Boro President
> Byrne to stop the planned construction.

May 2, 1928 – WANT COURT TO BAR TWO
FAMILY HOUSE

The Association made plans to institute
court proceedings to compel realty owners to
limit use of property to one family, which
members allege is supported by an early
deed. They are raising funds through $5
pledges.

April 17, 1930 – COURT UPHOLDS LEFFERTS
MANOR RESTRICTION EFFORT

Mrs. B.M. Wright ordered on Neighbor's
Plea not to take in Boarder. . . . Justice
Byrne in Supreme Court prevented Wright from
taking in boarders at 54 Midwood Street.
Neighbors discovered some months ago that
some of the occupants were not members of
the family or relatives. The neighbors
complained to the Lefferts Manor Association
and they went to court. The Association
pointed to the covenant of 1893. She pointed
to the changes. "You wouldn't know the old
place now." She replied with a sign hung
out in front that Negroes might buy or rent
her place if they chose. Her lawyer, Louis
Sacks, said "Others had actually changed
the appearance of their houses, while Mrs.
Wright's transgressions were not visible
from without." Frances Sullivan, counsel
for the Association, insisted that Mrs.
Wright could not by such defense void her
plain responsibility under the convenant.

May 30, 1938 – AREA IN FLATBUSH DEFENDS
ITS HERITAGE: "Commercialism Fails to Gain
Foothold in Lefferts Manor Community Where
Homeowner's Association is Ever on the Alert."

In an era of change and uncertainty,
really unique is "that tight little island"
which isn't an island at all but a highly
restricted residential section of Flatbush
where living conditions can never change--
The Lefferts Manor. In that area of ten
square blocks only one-family residences
may grace the scene. There are no shops,
no theaters, no places of amusement, no
miniature golf courses, no apartment houses.

Boarders are frankly frowned upon and private businesses are deplored.

Once an enterprising citizen thought to erect a swimming pool in the area. Such an idea was promptly dealt with, as have half a dozen other projects. This stern adherence to the one-family restriction has been upheld by the Lefferts Manor Association which has been organized for almost 20 years, carefully watching and maintaining the character of the neighborhood.

April 16, 1939 - COVENANT STILL HOLDS FORTH IN LEFFERTS MANOR NEIGHBORHOOD: "Civic Group Fights to Keep Restrictions to 1-Family Houses."

The quiet residential atmosphere of Brooklyn mourned by many as gone forever, still exists in a residential section of Flatbush. There in the Lefferts Manor, some of the city's prominent men and their families have found the refuge from the noise and congestion they sought. The Manor is the only residential neighborhood in the central metropolitan area which succeeded in completely maintaining its original bars against the changing conditions of the city. To insure this every purchaser was required to sign a covenant. Its enforcement, however, has succeeded only because of the vigilance of the Lefferts Manor Association. During the 20 years of the Association's life a variety of objectives has been accomplished. Its most important function, however, has been to protect the area's fundamental character.

Although court action has been taken in a score of cases, warnings have been sufficient to block most attempted violations of the covenant. In one case no less than 22 persons were living in a house formerly occupied by a family of four. Music studios, dress shops, and similar enterprises have sprung up now and then only to be closed upon discovery by the association. Sales of property for the construction of a public swimming pool and a large commercial parking lot were blocked; two boxing arenas nearby which disturbed the neighborhood's quiet were shut down shortly after they opened.

January 22, 1940 – LEFFERTS MANOR SECTION AGAIN IN COURT ROW: "Residents Seek Ban on Housing in Injunction Suit."

Another injunction suit in the long fight to keep the Lefferts Manor an exclusive residential section has been filed in Brooklyn Supreme Court. It is directed against Mrs. Laura Lloyd who in the complaint filed by Isaac Sargent, attorney for her neighbors, is accused of maintaining a rooming house at 82 Rutland Road and having a business sign in front of their house. The section contains the homes of many men who are leaders in business, banking and official circles.

December 17, 1941 – COURT OUSTS ROOMER FROM LEFFERTS MANOR

An injunction handed down by Supreme Court Justice Louis L. Fawcett, will dispossess boarders from the Lefferts Manor house at 65 Rutland Road owned by Amelia Lane.

June 8, 1950 – TRIAL SET ON ROOMING HOUSE BAN

Official Referee Peter P. Smith has scheduled for trial a suit that would permanently enjoin William Bernard Holmes, a post office clerk and his wife, Almeida, from using their two story and basement brownstone dwelling at 158 Rutland Road as a rooming house. The suit was brought by the Lefferts Manor Association. . . . Holmes acquired the property last August. On Oct. 1, according to papers filed in the case, he began advertising for roomers in the New York Amsterdam News. The Association then obtained from the court a temporary injunction restraining him from renting rooms until after the trial of the suit to make the permanent injunction.

June 19, 1950 - NO ROOMERS IN
LEFFERTS MANOR HOME

More than 125 persons overflowed the
tiny Borough Hall quarters of the Official
Supreme Court Referee Peter P. Smith when
the Lefferts Manor Association brought suit
to prevent a homeowner in the area from
using his house as a rooming house. After
some witnesses had been heard, Referee Smith
permanently enjoined William Bernard Holmes
and his wife Almeida from renting to roomers.

March 10, 1952 - MINISTER SEES
DISCRIMINATION IN HOLMES RENT CASE

The Rev. Carl Chworowsky of the Flatbush
Unitarian Church said last night that enjoin-
ing William B. Holmes from renting his
brownstone to roomers was a case of racial
discrimination, . . . he said that the action
was motivated by the fact that Holmes was a
Negro.

March 23, 1952 - DR. TAYLOR QUITS PROTEST
CAMPAIGN ON MANOR "BIAS"

The Rev. Dr. Gardner C. Taylor, pastor of
the Concord Baptist Church and President of
the Brooklyn Division of the Protestant
Council of the City of New York, it was
revealed today, has withdrawn from the
Holmes Defense Committee. . . . Dr. Taylor
is the third leading citizen of the Negro
community to withdraw sponsorship of the
committee's protest.

May 21, 1952 - BIAS COMMITTEE COLLAPSING

The Holmes Defense Committee appeared to
be near collapse today following the refusal
of the Rev. Sandy F. Ray and Mrs. Maude
Richardson to appear last night at a public
rally sponsored by the group. The with-
drawal of the two Negro leaders came on the
heels of an announcement that the Rev. Karl
Chworowsky and six other prominent Brooklyn
clergymen had also withdrawn from the
committee, after obtaining certain information. The information referred to was a

86

letter distributed by the Lefferts Manor
Association declaring the court action was
successfully prosecuted against 15 other
homeowners who had in the past violated
the covenant restricting homes to one-
family use. "The sole basis for prosecution
in each case was a violation of the restrictive covenant by the homeowner and not his
race, color or creed," the letter stated.
Members of the Association also pointed out
that at present seven Negro and one Chinese
family are living in the Lefferts Manor
area unmolested.

May 26, 1954 - CHIEF MULLS APPEAL FROM O.K.
OF LEFFERTS MANOR COVENANT

A Flatbush chef today considered an appeal
from a Brooklyn Supreme Court ruling which
upheld a prohibition against multi-family
dwellings in the Lefferts Manor section
near Ebbets Field. Official Referee John
B. Johnson last week upheld the legality
of the covenant written into deeds prior to
1900. The Lefferts Manor Association brought
suit against Ignatz Rabchenia, who purchased
the house at 150 Rutland Road for $15,000 in
1951. He claimed he spent $10,000 renovating
the structure from one-family to a multiple-
family dwelling. Referee Johnson decided
that the character of the area had not
changed since the covenants originally
were written into the deeds and thus cannot
be cancelled.

The legal battles of the Lefferts Manor Association to defend the community did not end in 1954, but
the Association's activities did disappear from
newspaper headlines. There seem to be three major
reasons for this loss of visibility. The first cause
is the folding of many of the major daily newspapers
in New York City, especially the Brooklyn Eagle.
The operation of the large number of dailies in New
York prior to 1960 resulted in considerable coverage
of "local" news. Today, local coverage is limited
to special items, or small sections of the New York
Times, Daily News and the New York Post. In addition
there are several neighborhood newspapers in
Brooklyn, but very few are dailies.

Secondly, the Lefferts Manor itself was subsumed
in the mind of the public into larger "neighborhood"
entities. The concept of neighborhood itself has
changed over the years, and the growth of city
planning and development movements resulted in the
creation of administratively meaningful communities
in which small enclaves have lost their unique
public identities. Whereas once Flatbush was a town
with many neighborhoods, it is now thought of as a
single neighborhood. At the same time, these new
large neighborhoods did not generate among their
members the same spirit of community as was associated with smaller, historically relevant neighborhood
units. Neighborhood community interest group
politics in the city has also changed. The larger,
more populous the unit--the more influence it wields.
"Neighborhood" leaders claim to speak for tens, if
not hundreds of thousands of people. The decade of
the sixties was also an era of the "politics of
confrontation" in which large segments of the city's
population, categorized ethnically, racially or
religiously, faced each other or the government in
a highly charged arena. Essentially, the small
neighborhood community became redundant in city
affairs.

Increasing Community Parameters

A new neighborhood group emerged on the local
scene in 1969--The Prospect-Lefferts-Gardens Neighborhood Association Incorporated. It was formed by
a small group of people with ideals and goals similar
to those of the Lefferts Manor Association (in fact,
most of the founders of the group were residents of
the Manor),but it was an organization with contemporary design and more comprehensive interests. The
original members strongly felt that racial integration
of the community could be accomplished without
destruction of the neighborhood, and in fact worked
to publicize the "positive" aspects of integrated
community life, an enormous challenge,given the
climate of the times. The new organization claimed
to represent a much larger collection of people,
more varied interests, and a larger geographic area
than the Lefferts Manor. The area it carved out
for itself included the Lefferts Manor, much to the
dismay of older, more conservative residents and the
Manor Association as well. The Manor has never
wished to involve itself with "outsiders." The new

88

group took a more activist position in regard to neighborhood problems, and was better able to capture the interest of city newspapers in their coverage of local events and issues. The Manor continued to be highlighted as a special place, but now only as a part of a wider community entity.

Both the continuation of some of the ideals of the Lefferts Manor and the blurring of its distinct social and geographic boundaries can be seen in the following newspapers story about Prospect-Lefferts-Gardens:

> February 27, 1974 - A FINE NEIGHBORHOOD
> IN PROSPECT
>
> "The quality of life has gone down in many parts of New York City," said Joseph Kolb, a brownstoner, "but here it has been maintained and in many ways improved. I don't think you will find another neighborhood like it--a stable, integrated area with architectural character."
> The neighborhood, located on the fringe of Crown Heights, is referred to as Flatbush by most residents. But the name Prospect-Lefferts-Gardens, given it by the neighborhood association, is slowly catching on and has been adopted by the city. "It's near Prospect Park, it takes in the old Lefferts homestead and it's near the Botanic Gardens," explained Mrs. Sealy. An estimated 25,000 to 30,000 people live in one and two family homes and low rise apartment houses in the area. . . . It includes the Lefferts Manor section in which Mrs. Sealy lives-- 592 houses many of them brownstone or white limestone, restricted by the original deed and city law to one-family occupancy. With graceful old-fashioned gas lights in front of the houses, some streets bear a strong resemblance to London's Chelsea section. Lefferts Manor residents want the Landmarks Preservation Commission to declare the section a historic district.[6]

The third reason for the decline of publicly visible actions of the Lefferts Manor Association to defend the sanctity of the community via the courts is the result of local population changes. To say

that the Association has maintained the same degree
of past vigilance would be false. Concomitant with
the influx of large numbers of nonwhite families in
the 1960s, older and prominent white members of the
Manor did relax their defenses, highlighting the
racial aspects of community definitions and the
social stigma of nonwhite groups. Also, the decade
of the 1960s was framed by civil rights movements,
during which "restrictive" covenants and "neighborhood preservation" groups were seen by liberal-minded
publics and political authorities as immoral, if not
illegal, racial barriers. The effect of this
attitude on the courts was to eliminate both real
and imagined racial discrimination. Subsequently
many city neighborhoods, defended by social class
hurdles, were quickly integrated, and the flight of
the white middle class out of the city was accelerated. Liberal-minded Manorites, for example, found
it unpalatable to defend their special community
against non-elite, mainly black invaders. Black
Manorites had even greater conflicts of conscience;
defending the exclusiveness of the Manor was seen as
a "racist" activity. So, for the most part blacks
avoided the Association and did not openly support
legal actions against violators of the covenant
lest they appear to be "Uncle Toms."

Despite the decrease in visibility, the
continuity of the goals of the Lefferts Manor
Association is reflected here in two pieces of
literature. The first, in 1938, lauded the decision
of the City Planning Commission which ruled against
apartment house construction in the Manor. In the
decision, A.A. Berle Jr., Commission Chairman, stated:
"There has been considerable feeling in the Commission
that there should be some areas of the city in which
individuals having the means can buy homes with some
assurance that the development of the district would
continue to be that of private, single-family
dwellings."

To celebrate, the Association published a
brochure, detailing the history of the Manor, and
distributed it to all members. The following "Message
from the President" captures the symbolic as well as
the practical importance of the restrictive covenant:

> The people of the Lefferts Manor live in
> a unique community. Here as if it were an
> island, is a tract of land covered with

homes, surrounded but unaffected by the
changing conditions to which other land
occupied by trade, business and multiple
dwellings is subject. . . . It is unusual
to have a situation such as this in a great
city like New York. This city, with its
cosmopolitan population, its active
industries, its commercial enterprises, is
in a constant state of flux. Real estate
values change with the changing uses of
property--the moving of retail centers, and
the inflow of other types of people. All
owners of real property and all those who
invest in mortgages, are affected by these
changes must be aware of them. To occupy
a home in an area stable in character and
destined to remain so throughout the years
is indeed a privilege.[7]

The brochure also included copies of the covenant
and an outline of the general form of the courts'
restraining orders in legal battles concerning violations of the restrictive covenant.

The second Lefferts Manor Association document,
published in 1971 and distributed since then to new
residents describes the goals of the organization and
solicits membership in the organization, which had
slowly decreased. The Association cited as its
immediate aims: "preventing the commercial use of
any Manor property, bringing people together for
their mutual acquaintance and enjoyment, improving
the general upkeep of the area, maintaining the one-
family covenant and protecting members' investment
in the community."

> KEY CONCERNS   Orderly and Safe Streets
>   Safe Traffic Conditions
>   Better Lighting
>   Proper Refuse Removal
>   Tree Conservation
>   Adequate Police Protection
>
> KEY GOALS   A distinctive and pleasurable
>   atmosphere; safe living con-
>   ditions; a stable community
>   without regard to race, creed
>   or color.[8]

In 1960 the Lefferts Manor area was zoned "one-
family only" by the New York City Planning Commission.

The designation was requested by the Lefferts Manor Association, as it was engaged then in constant litigation over the covenant. The zoning ordinance has added strength to the community's defense which at that time was beginning to waver. Since that time the Association has paid for the making of signs which loudly proclaim the zoning ordinance, and has had them hung from the street lamps in the Manor.

The Manor Association continues today to bring violators of the one-family, noncommercial covenant to court. However, blatant violations are not in evidence. The Association has since 1971 forced several commercial activities to cease in Manor homes and the simple threat of prosecution has eliminated some abuses of the community territory. Violations come to light when property is sold, as the violation must be removed before title to the property can be transferred.

During the fifty-year history of the Lefferts Manor as a completed community, the Manor Association and community members in general have fought many battles against their "enemies." The defensive position of the Manor can be organized into four categories as follows:

1. Because of the venerable history of the area, the ground upon which homes have been built is sacred. The residents, and the wider society, are morally bound to respect the symbolic value of the territory by not "desecrating" it through modification.

2. Legal recognition through the courts, and other official sanction of the symbolic meaning of the territory, such as zoning and landmarks status, has been sought and obtained.

3. The public argument that for the city as a whole to survive, it needs to retain and attract rich, powerful and prominent people. This can be done by providing them with protected enclaves.

4. The conviction that discrimination in American society which is based on social class or economic situation is neither illegal nor immoral. The Lefferts Manor discriminates by class.

Similarly, the "enemies" of the exclusive character of the Manor have respectively four offensive arguments which they use to undermine the special nature of the community.

1. The social class snobbishness of the Manor is contrary to the egalitarian values of American society.

2. The restrictive covenant of the Lefferts Manor differentially affects various ethnic, racial and religious groups. Therefore, selection of Manorites results in de facto discrimination on these grounds.

3. Individual rights to exploit property are more important, and constitutionally protected than are historical, communal values and privileges.

4. The Lefferts Manor community is no longer the super-exclusive section that it once was. The area has changed over the years; therefore the legal and social rules protecting its special character are no longer valid.

All these defensive and offensive postures have been used since the Manor was established, in the courts, in public statements and in private arguments. More and more, however, the integrity of the Lefferts Manor is threatened by forces which cannot be thwarted by historical and communal values. Mortgage and insurance red-lining, the general economic decline of the city as a whole and the pervasiveness of the feeling that city living, per se, is undesirable are the issues that have at present the greatest impact on the future of the Manor and other stable inner city neighborhoods. Housing abandonment, property tax arrears, street crime, arson and frustration are a few of the manifestations of these problems which will be discussed in later chapters.

The following "Message from the President" of the Lefferts Manor Association in 1978 indicates both similarities and differences with the Presidential Message of 1938. The rapid changes which occurred in the 1970s have left their mark on the Association which now must reluctantly recognize that the well-being of this middle-class "island" depends more and more on the stability of surrounding, less affluent areas. The last paragraph of the message, however, emphasizes the classic Manorite independence.

MESSAGE FROM THE PRESIDENT
LEFFERTS MANOR VOICE (Autumn 1978)

Lefferts Manor is a very special neighborhood. It is special because it is a neighborhood which, in the midst of much change and turmoil in the borough, has held itself together by working together.

The beauty, charm, and stateliness which is Lefferts Manor today is no accident. It is the happy, planned result of neighbors working together and helping one another year after year in an intelligent and common-sense way.

We on the Board of the Lefferts Manor Association want to blend the successes and traditions of the past with the changes and challenges of the future. We recognize that Lefferts Manor must increasingly concern itself with the problems of adjoining areas, both commercial and residential. And that's what we are doing now, and with your help, hope to continue to do in the future. . . .

Remember, all of our support comes from within the community and not from outside foundations or agencies. And that's very important. It means that you, our contributors and workers, are the only ones to whom we have to account in justify-ing our various projects for the community.

Chapter IV

INVASION AND SUCCESSION

Attractions

Urbanization and ethnic succession are problems
that most city communities cannot avoid. The effects
of these processes on different neighborhoods are not
necessarily the same. For example, the Lefferts
Manor was relatively well protected from the otherwise overwhelming high density residential construction in Central Brooklyn. Historical decisions and
political influence had insured its future as a
special community, and it continued to attract people
who thought of themselves as special as well. The
ripple effect of the Manor's desirability also had
a positive effect on the rest of the Prospect-
Lefferts-Gardens area. The Manor and other
"urbanized suburbs" continue to function as
"dormitory communities" within the political
boundaries of the city.[1]

In a way the Lefferts Manor has been provided
with the "best of all possible" urban worlds (to
paraphrase Professor Pangloss) by the recreational
and cultural institutions that were part of Olmstead
and Vaux's 1866 urban plan. Illustration 2 outlines
these amenities in relation to the Manor. Prospect
Park, a block away from the Lefferts Manor, provides
many acres of meadows, woods and urban gardens.
Supplementing these attractions in the park are
band concerts, "Opera in the Park," boating, a zoo,
ice skating and horseback riding. Also near to the
Manor is the extensive Brooklyn Botanical Garden.
The Garden opened in 1910 and today offers many
horticultural delights including exotic green-
houses, world famous Japanese gardens, a magnificent cherry orchard, and quiet, contemplative rose
gardens. The Brooklyn Museum and Art Institute
opened its doors to the public in 1890 and continues
to be a world renowned art center with excellent
collections of ancient as well as modern art. The
museum also features concerts, lectures, films, an
art school, and special exhibits brought to the
museum from all over the world. The Central Branch
of the Brooklyn Public Library completes the area's

Illustration 2. THE HUB OF VAUX AND OLMSTEAD'S CITY PLAN

0. Grand Army Plaza
1. Main Branch Brooklyn Public Library
2. Brooklyn Museum
3. Brooklyn Botanic Gardens
4. Brooklyn Zoo

cultural complex. It was also opened in 1890, but the original structure was gradually replaced by a large modernistic building between 1912 and 1940. The Library is situated on Grand Army Plaza, which was the center of Olmstead and Vaux's plan of radiating boulevards. The Plaza includes a bronze sculptured fountain and a large memorial arch--the Soldiers and Sailors Monument--which was erected as a memorial to the Civil War dead in 1871.

The residential boulevard, Eastern Parkway, begins at the Grand Army Plaza. At the southern end of Prospect Park is the Parade Grounds which serves today as a baseball, football and tennis center. A second residential parkway, Ocean Parkway, leads out from the Parade Grounds to Brighton Beach, and like Eastern Parkway, has traditionally been an attraction for Brooklyn's upper middle class. In sum, the Lefferts Manor has been able to maintain its high symbolic value and to continue to attract people seeking respectable urban homes while the city as a whole began losing these people to suburban migration.

There are other important historical factors which have positively influenced the shape, composition and reputation of the Manor. The once nationally famous baseball stadium, and Brooklyn institution, Ebbets Field, opened only a few blocks away from the Manor in 1912. Although it might seem at first that this kind of facility would adversely affect neighboring residential areas, Ebbets Field had the opposite effect. While the stadium did attract large numbers of fans who created occasional headaches for local homeowners, it also insured that more noxious industrial and commercial uses of the territory would be prevented for a time. The building of the popular sports center near the Manor in addition fostered a spin-off of other entertain- ment and recreational establishments in the community. Of greatest importance, during the tenure of the Brooklyn Dodgers at Ebbets Field, numerous nightclubs and restaurants flourished on the avenues near the Manor and bolstered the commercial vitality of the streets. Manorites were within walking distance of seeing the team that was the "Pride of Brooklyn," and also dining at the highly touted restaurants and supper clubs. Well-to-do patrons and even theater-goers from Manhattan, would travel to Flatbush in cabs and

limousines for the night life there. Flatbush
Avenue, near the Manor in the 1920, 30s, 40s and
part of the 50s, was an "in" place.

The quality of design and construction of
Manor homes continue to have significant impact on
the symbolic and economic value of the Lefferts
Manor. Manor homes were built between 1890 and
1920 by prominent urban architects which resulted in
a delightful mix of attached, semi-attached and
detached homes, suburban-style mansions, rows of
brick townhouses, imposing brownstones and limestone
structures. Victorian wood-frame houses, bedecked
with turrets, gables and wide porches; Tudor style
row houses; Queen Anne Revival brownstones; neo-
classical and Revival Georgetown brick and sculptured limestone add to the Manor's eclectic urban
panorama. The "look" of the Lefferts Manor is not
the monotonous vision of row upon row of identical
houses such as that found on many city streets.

What the Lefferts Manor was not is here
described by Edith Wharton in her autobiography,
A Little Girl's New York:

> In those days the little "brownstone houses"
> (I never knew the technical name of the geo-
> logical horror) marched up Fifth Avenue . . .
> in an almost unbroken procession from
> Washington Square to the Central Park . . .
> all with Dutch "stoops" (the five or six
> steps leading to the front door), and all
> not more than three stories high, marched
> Parkward in an orderly procession, like a
> young ladies boarding school taking its
> daily exercise. The facades varied in
> width from twenty to thirty feet, and here
> and there, but rarely, the line was broken
> by a brick home with brownstone trimmings;
> but otherwise they were all so much alike
> that one could understand how easily it
> would be for a dinner guest to go to the
> wrong house--as once befell a timid young
> girl of eighteen, to whom a vulgar nouveau
> riche hostess revealed her mistake, turning
> her out carriageless into the snow. (1969:
> 60)

Edith Wharton goes on, in her urban polemic, to
correlate the architecture of homes to the kinds of

people within them by saying that: "The lives behind the brownstone fronts were, with few exceptions, as monotonous as their architecture." Uniform, mass-produced neighborhoods were not for the urban elite. Wharton's common-sense grasp of the interaction between physical structures and the people who use them is remarkable. It is interesting to note in this vein that similar reflections have been made by social scientists about the personalities and social lives of people who live in uniform suburban communities. The "ordinary" middle-class person of the 1970s is similar to the 1920 counterpart--a status seeker who cannot afford the "real thing" and must settle for an imitation of symbols of prestige, hence the quarter acre "estate."[2]

The interiors of Manor homes were also executed in such a way as to avoid duplication, even in those homes with similar exterior form. Each house was to be a "personal" dwelling that would reflect the character of the owner. This personification was shown in resales of homes; the new owner would invariably destroy some perfectly adequate interior feature in order to add their own individual mark to the structure. The construction techniques and building materials employed in building homes in the Manor insured that their original values would be lasting. Sturdy brick and stone walls, heavy, closely set cross-beams, ceilings with sculptured plaster detailing, stained and leaded glass windows, parquet floors of oak laid over hardwood sub-flooring, oak and mahogany wood panelling, matching built-in cabinets, beamed dining room ceilings, spacious rooms and libraries, marble tiled bathrooms, porcelain and marble sinks, solid brass plumbing--all these things went into the construction of a Manor home. One need only look closely at the materials used in building modern homes, or to observe workmen putting up, or rather slapping together, today's housing to realize how exceptional are the Lefferts Manor houses. They cannot be replaced today, but the people who live within them can be replaced. Ultimately the viability of the Manor rests not on the physical structure of the community, but on the people who come to live within it.

Clarence Day's Father could easily have been a Manorite. In this excerpt from Life with Father, we see a literary version of the social-psychology of neighborhood transition. In the 1870s every "respectable" citizen of Manhattan owned his own home. The general requirements were a solid three- or four-story house, without a mortgage and located within a few blocks of Fifth Avenue--between Fifty-Ninth Street and Washington Square. It should be noted that these were the very homes despised by Edith Wahrton in her biography. Clarence Day's father looked around carefully and bought a house at 420 Madison Avenue:

> This was a sunny house, just below Forty-ninth Street. It was fairly near Central Park, and it was in a new and eligible district for good private residences. Brokers said that "the permanent residential quality of the whole section" was guaranteed by the fine public edifices which have been built in the neighborhood. . . .
>
> For the first ten or fifteen years that we lived at 420, the neighborhood got better and better, Father's judgement as to its permanence seemed to be justified. It had become thickly planted with residences in which many friends of our family were making their homes. We had grown fond of 420 by that time. Birth and death and endless household events had taken place inside its walls, and it had become part of ourselves.
>
> Then business began invading upper Fifth Avenue and spreading to Madison. A butcher bought a house near us and turned it into a market. We felt he was an impudent person and bought nothing from him for months, until in an emergency Mother sent me there for a rack of lamb chops. We then discovered that this butcher was not only an upstart, he was expensive and he was catering to the fashionable Fifth Avenue families and didn't care a rap about ours.
>
> More and more of the old houses around us were made into stores. After 1900 some of the best people left, and soon the whole district began steadily sliding down hill. (1969:74-78)

It is of great importance to notice in this piece the strong attachment of the Day family to their residence, and the personal loss that was felt as their neighborhood began to change. Again, as in so many other cases of urban decline in residential areas, the encroachment of commercial activity is the major culprit. This situation points out the importance of the Lefferts Manor restrictive covenant in maintaining the symbolic stability of the community.

Invaders

The following pages sketch the different waves of people who came into the Lefferts Manor and Prospect-Lefferts-Gardens area after the Manor was established as a first-class urban neighborhood. All of these people have contributed to the physical and symbolic content of the present community. Included in this section are groups and individuals who are best described as "co-presents" to Manorites: residents of the area who Manorites would not be willing to include as part of the community's social inventory. Co-presents, and residents of other neighborhoods close to the Manor have also had significant impact on the value of the Lefferts Manor community, both negatively and positively. In the pages that follow the relationship between self and group identities, and the community in which one lives, is emphasized.

Irish and Italian Catholics

Between 1890 and 1950, local Irish and Italian Catholics were to Manorites what Jacob Riis's "Other Half" and O'Henry's "Four Million" were to the city's elite society: summarily, the unwashed, lower caste of Brooklyn. In Prospect-Lefferts-Gardens, Irish Catholics were originally sequestered on the eastern side of Rogers Avenue, the western boundary of the Lefferts Manor, which is symbolically the "other side of the tracks." All American large cities and small towns have equivalent physical boundaries to signify social distances between classes and ethnic groups.[3]

There are other geographical expressions of social distance and power in the community which have remained relatively stable in the community over the years. These expressions are shown in Map 12. For example, the religious hierarchy in the area, circa 1920, was demonstrated by the sites of local dominant Protestant churches. If we think of these churches as being at relative distances from

101

Map 12. LEFFERTS MANOR ENVIRONS

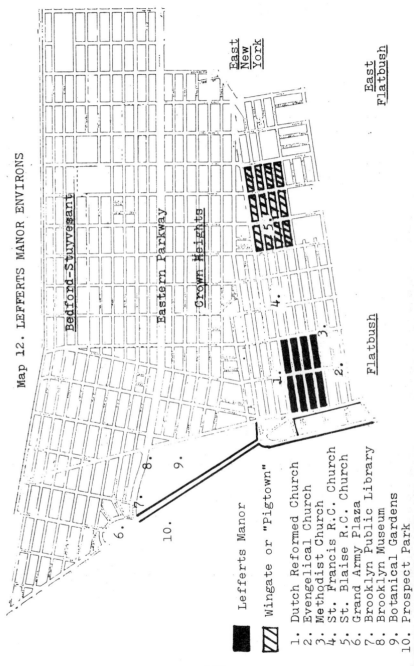

Bedford-Stuyvesant

Eastern Parkway

Crown Heights

East
New
York

East
Flatbush

Flatbush

■ Lefferts Manor

▨ Wingate or "Pigtown"

1. Dutch Reformed Church
2. Evengelical Church
3. Methodist Church
4. St. Francis R.C. Church
5. St. Blaise R.C. Church
6. Grand Army Plaza
7. Brooklyn Public Library
8. Brooklyn Museum
9. Botanical Gardens
10. Prospect Park

the center of the Lefferts Manor, we discover that
the Dutch Reformed, Evangelical and Methodist churches
are all located near the restricted boundaries of the
Manor. The Reformed and Methodist churches have
continued to alternate as meeting places for the
Manor Association's annual gatherings.

On the "other side of the tracks" (Rogers
Avenue) we find the Roman Catholic church, St.
Francis, which was originally dominated by Irish
parishioners, as it is today by black West Indians.
In 1955, another Roman Catholic church, St. Blaise,
was built further eastward to serve Wingate, a
working-class Italian section. Before the opening
of St. Blaise, Italians would travel several blocks
south of their community for services at a church
with Italian clergy, even though they lived closer
to St. Francis. Italians who lived in Wingate in
the early days of its history recall that it was
referred to as "Pig Town." The name, they say, was
given to the area because of the small farms
operating there, some of which had pigs and other
animals. Until 1970, there remained a poultry
processing plant in Wingate. The section is still
zoned for light industrial activity and contains a
few scrap yards, as well as a mixture of plumbing,
auto supply and service shops, and other manual
trade establishments. It is therefore a "mixed
use" community, typical of many working-class or
blue-collar ethnic neighborhoods in the city.
Wingate at present is a low-density area with an
interesting mix of a small number of Italian and
many black homeowners and renters.

The historical antipathy between Irish and
Italian Catholics in the neighborhood is recounted
by people in terms of the hostility expressed
towards Italians at St. Francis church. Italian
adults were not welcome at services and Italian
children experienced many difficulties if they were
fortunate enough to be admitted to the parochial
grade school. Competition between lower caste
ethnic groups has always been common to city life.
Today, new low caste ethics--blacks, Hispanics and
Asians--frequently battle over control of local
institutions, influence in government social
service programs, as well as the traditional power
over local "turf."

The situation at St. Francis changed later as the Irish middle class was one of the first groups to begin moving out of the area about 1950. This exodus created financial problems for the parish and resulted in a warmer reception to local Italians. But Italians who attended St. Francis's grammar school in the 1950s remember still being mistreated by students and "religious" teachers alike. The acceptance of Italians was only a grudging acceptance. The reason why parents sent their children to private and parochial schools in those years is the same as the reason given today: to keep their children safe from the lower-class children who attend public schools.

The persistence of the "Pig Town" label for the Italian community was demonstrated in 1978 as I spoke to a college student who once lived in Prospect-Lefferts-Gardens. Speaking of research on his ex-community, I asked if he knew one of the persons interviewed who was Italian. The student who was Irish responded, "Oh no. He must have lived in Pig Town."

The Irish Catholic section of the area was more residentially and commercially developed than that of the Italians. In the Irish sector there were more apartment houses, stores and more substantial one- and two-family homes. It was also a "better" place because it had no vacant lots, scrap yards or shacks such as those that could be found in Wingate. Still the Irish part of the community was merely a lower-class enclave. It was literally nearer to the Lefferts Manor, but figuratively many miles away. Even today there are few Manorites who are familiar with the streets or people who passed their eastern borders.

Long-term Italian and Irish Catholic residents of Prospect-Lefferts-Gardens today, but not in the Lefferts Manor, still speak of the Manor as the bastion of the rich and the powerful. They remember the wealthy and prominent Manorites--politicians, bankers, judges, lawyers and doctors. Unfortunately, many of these old-time residents feel that the area has been "ruined" by blacks, but they still have a great deal of nostalgia for the Manor. They can tell you of the times they walked through the Manor as youngsters and were awed by the large houses, gardens, fancy cars, uniformed servants and other

104

symbols of affluence. Most of these residual,
working-class area residents never had had an opportunity to see the inside of a Lefferts Manor house
until the Prospect-Lefferts-Gardens Neighborhood
Association began holding "house tours" in an attempt
to interest people in buying houses in the community.
The tours themselves were an Association tactic to
counter the image that the neighborhood was severely
deteriorated. The Lefferts Manor Association, being
more staid, was generally against the tours within
their boundaries. They felt that activities open to
the general public would bring "riff raff" into the
community.

The Lefferts Manor, to lower caste oldtimers,
was a distant goal. When a few finally "made it"
and moved into their dream community, they wanted to
preserve the distance between themselves and their
less fortunate ethnics. They believed that an
important part of what they had attained through
social mobility was the "right" to that social
distance. They did not Italianize or Gaelicize
the Manor. They changed their ethnic lifestyles and
dissociated themselves from less upwardly mobile friends
and relatives who lived in nearby areas. They
accepted the social values and mannerisms of the
indigenous Manorites. These invaders were, in all
probability, converted to the Manor way of life
prior to their ascendancy through a process of
anticipatory socialization. Such pre-socialization
is an integral part of mobility aspirations in
American society. In many cases, like the "Black
Bourgeoisie" so effectively described by E. Franklin
Frazier, the lower-caste Manorites became "more
royal than the king."[4] There were to be no Italian
feasts and no Irish wakes in the Lefferts Manor.
Until 1971, the Lefferts Manor Association officially
frowned upon "block parties" and other street activities as were typical historically of New York's
working-class communities. Association officers
have generally argued that these kinds of public
activities were contrary to the character of the
community that they were trying to maintain.

Jews

The Irish, Italian and other middle-class
Catholics who managed to slip into the Manor slowly
over the years became part of the community's social

fabric, as all invaders eventually do. The Catholic
achievers and their more established Protestant neighbors in the Manor became disturbed in the 1930s when
large numbers of middle-class Jewish achievers started
moving toward the Lefferts Manor from other parts of
Brooklyn and New York City. The geographic route
to the Manor by middle-class Jews is almost identical
to that taken by blacks thirty years later: from
Manhattan, to Bedford-Stuyvesant, to Crown Heights,
and then to Flatbush. The desire of socially mobile
Jews to move to residential settings that reflected
their personal accomplishments is best exemplified
by the following discussion from Gerald Green's
classic, The Last Angry Man. In this selection, Dr.
Sam Abelman tries to explain to his family why he
wants to buy a particular house. The street he
speaks of, incidentally, is in a residential section
of Crown Heights which has attached to it great
historical and symbolic notability. It is also only
seven blocks north of the Lefferts Manor.

"So you bought a house, did you?" Sarah
asked. "Which one, the seventeen-room
mansion on Crown Street that needed four
thousand dollars worth of repair? Or the
one on Union Street where the roof leaked?
What lemon did Dannenfelser unload on you,
realty expert?"
"Okay so you know!" the doctor shouted.
"To hell with it! I wanted a new house
in a respectable neighborhood and I got
it. It's the semi-detached three-story
brownstone on Republic Street, and I got
it for a steal! I'm not backing out and
I'm not asking a red cent from anyone to
help me get it! Not a word out of you
Sarah! You've stopped me long enough
from doing things I want--"
"At your age," she said primly, "doing
maintenance on a house that size. With a
tenant yet!"
"Pop, pop, it's not for you," Harry
Platt pleaded. "I've looked it over and
I know."
"At least go on the television show and
take Mr. Thrasher's money," Eunice implored
him. "Then it won't be so bad."
"What do you know?" the doctor cried.
"What do all of you know? I'm doing it my
way this time. I've lived too long to

worry about it, and I don't have too long
to go. I want to die in a house that looks
like a doctor's house, not a goddamn slum
surrounding the scum of the earth, who are
my darling patients, if you please." (1956:
397)

Some of the Jewish pioneers who moved into the
Manor in the 1930s and 1940s tell of open and more
veiled anti-Semitism directed toward them by
established Manorites. One person interviewed told
a story that well represents upper-middle-class
"respectable" bigotry practices. It is necessary
for ethnic scholars to realize that respectable
people do not use common methods to put people in
their places. America's Manorites do not stone
people, burn crosses, or fire-bomb houses. However,
because genteel citizens do not participate in the
ordinary repertoire of expressing prejudice, this
does not mean that they are less demented than their
working-class cousins. The Jewish pioneer spoke of
an incident which took place in 1950, and involved
her seven year old daughter. Occasionally, the child
played with a Gentile neighbor's daughter. One day
her child came home to say that she had been invited
to her friend's birthday party.

As the parents of the children were not on
speaking terms, the invitation was never formally
confirmed. On the afternoon of the party, the little
girl was prettily dressed by her mother and hesitantly
sent off to the party with a gift for her friend.
When she arrived at the door, she was politely
refused entry by the maid, and came home to her
mother in tears. Examples such as this, of ethnic,
racial and religious discrimination in Manor social
life are often repeated by the invaders with whom
I spoke. The only major changes in scripts are the
respective ethnic, racial and religious identities
of the "victims" and "villains."

Veterans: Undesirable Heroes

After the end of the Second World War in 1945,
there was a severe housing shortage and apartment
shortage in New York City. During the war the construction of new dwelling units was at a standstill,
while older buildings were allowed to deteriorate.
Over 300,000 servicemen from Brooklyn returned home

107

after the conflict and most sought to set up their
own households. Many new families came on the scene
as marriages took place after being postponed for the
duration of the war. Due to the housing shortage, some
of the veterans tried to buy Manor houses and use them
for more than single-family occupancy. For the most
part, the veterans were white and of various ethnic
backgrounds, but to Manorites they lacked adequate
social class pedigrees. The Lefferts Manor Association viewed the veterans as "dangerous," and thought
that they were trying to "ruin the neighborhood."
The Association bitterly fought, and won, the battle
against the ex-servicemen.

There is an interesting postscript to this
incident. As time passed, many Manorites began to
express some regrets about keeping the veterans out
of the community. Thirty years later, older Manorites
who were active in the Association at that time, and
who reflect on the changes they have seen in the
community, are likely to admit that perhaps they were
wrong: "at least the veterans were white."

Blacks and the Special Problems
of Nonwhite Invaders

During the 1950s the white residents of the
Lefferts Manor, of all ethnic and religious persua-
sions, overcame their differences, temporarily, to
oppose the influx of middle-class blacks who wanted
to move into the Manor, and who already had bought
homes in surrounding neighborhoods. Again, as one
speaks to older black Manorites the all-too-familiar
tales of discrimination, and the pain that individuals
felt in those years comes to the surface. The
stories are stylized echoes of organized group, and
random individual hostility toward newcomers, who
are seen as potential threats to the definition of
the Manor as a sacred and exalted place.

One black resident related how, many years
ago, he passed by the Manor on his way to work. He
rode the trolley car that ran down Flatbush Avenue
on the western edge of the area. He remembered how
beautiful the community looked then, as he peered
down the Manor streets. He and his wife dreamed of
the day that they would be able to afford to live
in such a neighborhood. About twelve years later,
in 1960, he and his family achieved their goal

and moved into the Lefferts Manor, only to be met by
quiet viciousness from his new neighbors. Most of
the Manorites gave him and his wife the"silent treatment." They weathered the silent abuse, but over the
years have made very few friends locally. Unfortunately, for one that most would like to see as an
"heroic" character, he as other Manorites, later
felt that the community was being threatened by
other newcomers and he joined with his neighbors
to keep "them" out.

The first reaction to threat to the community
from invading forces seems to be an attempt, feeble
or strong, to keep out new members. Only as a last
resort do Manorites turn to flight. This flight
from the Manor takes place not during the present,
but in future generations. It is the children of
the Manor who move away. Over the fifty-year
history of the Lefferts Manor there has only been a
very slow rate of turnover. Here the circle turns
ever so slowly.

Some of the black pioneers in the Lefferts Manor
evidence resentment over the fact that the neighborhood is now predominately black. The causes of
their resentment are complex. Most have moved from
other areas of the city that were virtually all black.
After attaining middle-class status, they desired
to move into a white or "integrated" community.
Later they found that an "integrated" community is
merely one that is changing from white to black.
Their explanations for wanting to relocate in white
areas are universal. A common theme is that past
experience has taught them that in black neighborhoods
there is a gradual decrease in the quality and quantity of city services--sanitation, police, and protection from landlord abuses and real estate specula-
tion. The abandonment by city authorities of black
neighborhoods, they saw, led to the growth of slums
in what were once stable, middle-class neighborhoods.

From interviews, it is apparent that white
people are desirable neighbors, not so much because
blacks raise their social status by living near them
(although for some this may be the case), but because
blacks feel that the presence of whites will protect
them from abuse by whites and white institutions.
The great fear that black Manorites have is that
once the community is all black, it will no longer
enjoy its special historical relationship with city

authorities. Until 1978, with the Manor having a
majority of black residents, the community was still
perceived by its residents as receiving adequate, if
not more than adequate, city services. The slight
decrease in the quality of these services in the
past few years, however, has been automatically
correlated with the growing number of nonwhites
in the area. In general, whites see nonwhites as
the direct cause, and nonwhites see themselves as
more indirect causes of the decline in neighborhood
appearance and viability. Since 1978 one would be
hard pressed to find anyone who is satisfied with
the delivery of city services.

Adding to the great degree of ethnic diversity
in the Prospect-Lefferts-Gardens area, due in large
part to the slow rate of ethnic succession which
leaves segments of ethnic cohorts behind, have been
earlier and more recent mini-invasions of West
Indian, and other blacks from the Caribbean, Central
America and South America. More recently, Hispanics
and Asians have been moving into the blocks on the
periphery of the Manor. Few of these last two
groups have bought homes in the Manor itself.

Some unusual community-related problems have
developed because of the expressive cultural values
of Islanders who have bought Manor homes. They seem,
for example, to be unwilling to accept the conservative, Victorian-American visual traditions of the
community, and are also seen to form exclusive ethnic
and family cliques. This last charge against them
was similarly lodged against Jews and Italians who
came into the Manor during the earlier history.
The self and externally imposed isolation of the
Islanders from Manor institutions may protect them
for a time from exposure to the Lefferts Manor
culture of community, but eventually they too will
be assimilated.

The bright colors and decorations that some
Islanders apply to their homes are seen by more
established residents as affronts to the subdued
ambience that pervades the Manor streets. Fronts
of houses are considered to be symbolic community
property which reflects on the status of everyone.
Individuals are not seen as having the "right" to
mar the face of the community. Not only have a few
Islanders not internalized the particular staid
culture of community in the Manor; they have not

been acculturated to the generally demure versions of the American upper-middle-class neighborhood. Their family and ethnic celebrations, for example, begin late at night and go on to early morning hours, prompting older Manorites to make anonymous phone calls to the celebrants and, on occasion, the local police precinct.

These cultural conflicts in the Manor also lead to intraracial as well as interracial conflicts; American black Manorites feel that Islanders give blacks in general a "bad name." On the other hand, Islanders, many of whom accept the negative stereotype of poor southern and urban American blacks, feel that "they" have given "them" a bad name. Whites who observe this lack of communality between black people from different cultures, see these comments as support for their own racial biases. The more racist among them give these differences as evidence that "even blacks don't like blacks." Such intragroup hostility is typical in American ethnic society as successful Reform Jews dissociate themselves from the orthodox, Irish elites from the "Shanty Irish" and Italian "prominenti" from their working-class co-ethnics.

Back to City Brownstoners: A Confused Invasion

In 1969 there began a new invasion into the Lefferts Manor and some nearby streets. These invaders are part of New York City's Brownstone Revival movement which has been slowly growing. The movement consists mainly of white upper-middle-class urbanites who are seeking to save for themselves the remaining historically and architecturally valuable residential properties in the city. This movement has been relatively successful in the renaissance of such neighborhoods as the upper west side of Manhattan, Brooklyn Heights and Park Slope in Brooklyn. Similar brownstone invasions have occurred in New Orleans, Mobile, San Francisco, Baltimore, Chicago, Boston and other cities with substantial inventories of culturally valuable housing "captured" within the central city. The movement is often referred to more generally and nationally as the "Back to City" movement. Social critics call it "gentrification" or "displacement."

The complexity of motives for brownstoning is
of interest to us only in so far as they relate to
the aspirations of relatively well-to-do people to
retake from the not-so-well-to-do, the inner city
neighborhoods that their parents may have abandoned
a generation ago. There are many historical periods
that are favored by these new city neighborhood
affecionados. Because most of New York's Colonial
and Federal housing has disappeared, Victorian Period
homes, such as those in the Manor, are in great demand.
Sample renderings of these desirables were given in
Illustration 3. It appears that the brownstoner has
combined the physical appearance and symbolic
meanings of venerated historical epochs with the
ideal version of the American community. The movement expresses the desire of people to recreate and
preserve traditional middle-class residential values
in the face of the general assault against community
life in the nation's cities. A more cynical, yet
sympathetic, evaluation of the people who participate
in this movement has been provided by impressario Sol
Yurick who lived in the Park Slope neighborhood as it
experienced this unusual neighborhood transition.

> What kind of people are these, the invading
> army? Lawyers and professors and doctors
> and architects and psychologists and social
> workers and writers and newspapermen and city
> officials and Mayor Lindsay's daughter and
> poverty fund richies who've made the transi-
> tion from idealism to hustler and investment
> analysts and artists and teachers. Is this
> an army? Is that fair? They're only people,
> you see, like you and me, with feelings and
> individual anxieties, desiring humanity,
> expression and love. They're of liberal
> temperament and they've backed all the right
> causes from Kennedy to anti-pollution to
> integration.[5]

With the respect for history and culture brownstoners
seem to have, it is not difficult to understand why
some Manorites have taken the invaders as potential
saviors for the fading fashionable character of the
community. The values of the brownstoners and the
Manorites are similar, but as could be expected, they are
not embraced by all those who live in the Lefferts
Manor. One source of hostility to these new invaders
are more racially militant blacks, and sympathetic
whites, who see the movement as a refined version

Illustration 3. VARIETIES OF CLASSIC URBAN HOUSING.

of "negro removal." An interesting analysis and
description of the "negro removal" process is provided here by Frances Fox Piven and Richard A.
Cloward:

> Other federal programs, such as urban
> renewal, were turned against blacks;
> renewal projects were undertaken in most
> big cities to deal with the black invasion
> through "slum clearance," by reclaiming
> land taken by the expanding ghettoes and
> restoring it to "higher economic" use (i.e.,
> to uses that would keep whites and businesses
> in the central city)....
> . . . seventy percent of the families thus
> uprooted were black. . . . But with local
> blacks becoming more disorderly and more
> demanding in the early 1960s, local govern-
> ment began to make some concessions. Urban
> renewal provides one example. By the 1960s,
> black protests were mounting against "Negro
> Removal" in the guise of "slum clearance."
> (1971:241-42)

According to a report of the National Urban
Coalition in 1978, if you are elderly poor, or working
class and live in an area underoing rehabilitation, or
in a suddenly fashionable neighborhood, you are a prime
candidate for displacement by well-to-do suburbanites
longing for the city life they left behind. The
Coalition's study of forty-four cities showed that
over half of the rehabilitated neighborhoods had
higher minority populations before rehabilitation
began.[6]

Even those in the Manor who protest the in-
migration of whites do so as respectfully as possible.
They would not raise their voices in order to stem
the movement of whites into the Manor. Typically,
brownstoners are given the Manor "cold shoulder."
One more enterprising black resident put a sign in
his window during a Prospect-Lefferts-Gardens
Neighborhood Association house tour which announced:
"White racists--This House Is Not For Sale." Others
try to be as rude as is possible when whites come to
inspect Manor houses which are on the market.

Homeowners and real estate agents still exercise
the power to choose to whom homes are shown, and a
"black market" in Manor housing has developed, or

rather continued. In Brooklyn neighborhoods, screening of prospective homeowners is accomplished by informal advertising in ethnic and other media with "acceptable" audiences. Also, more discriminating real estate offices are contacted to help sell Manor homes. Whites who wish to discriminate against blacks, and blacks who want only whites to move into the community to maintain a presence, accomplish their goals in similar fashion by creating, so to speak, a "white market" in Manor houses.

These illegal, immoral, unethical, but culturally acceptable, practices of racial discrimination have apparent economic benefits that often overwhelm racial pride. Nonwhites and brownstoners are the most likely groups to pay inflated prices for local housing; brownstoners because of the limited quantity of architecturally suitable property, and nonwhites, because of their historically restricted access to decent housing due to city-wide discrimination and racial steering in real estate. Yearly studies of discrimination in home sales by public and private agencies in New York have consistently shown that white and black prospective homebuyers are directed toward different areas, even if they are of the same socio-economic status.

Blacks and brownstoners are therefore in direct ecological competition with each other in many city neighborhoods, and in cities in general that are experiencing the "Back to City" movement. We should expect that some of the future confrontations between these groups will take on violent aspects. There have already been incidents of personal violence against middle-class white brownstoners who have invaded lower- or lower-middle-class neighborhoods. Most have been recorded as ordinary crimes of violence, but one cannot help but feel that they have had a great deal to do with the feelings of black adolescents that their "turf" has been violated. Eventually brownstoners in city neighborhoods, if the phenomenon continues, will demand extraordinary protection from city authorities to protect them from the "natives" of their adopted communities. And if cities are interested in promoting the back-to-city movement as a way to replace its depleted middle-class population, such measures must be adopted. Even the rejuvenation of American cities, then, presents some thorny social, moral and political problems that will develop from this new form of class warfare.

Although violence against brownstoners has not
occurred within the Manor, there have been several
reports of problems with local teenagers outside the
Manor boundaries, where the invaders have displaced
nonwhite families, often renters. Frequently, when a
brownstoner buys a house in the inner city for single-
family or two-family use, the house has been occupied
for many years by several hard-pressed families, or
many more single-room occupants. The resentment of
the displaced, or their neighborhood friends, when
they are put out on the street often lingers for
long periods of time. The brownstoners then become
a symbol to minority youth of a new kind of oppression, which can result in harassment and intimidation.
Many blacks also see the situation as, so to speak,
"putting the shoe on the other foot."

It should be expected that even middle-class
brownstoners would experience some instances of
prejudice and discrimination within the Manor as did
earlier invaders. There is always "something wrong"
with newcomers to any community. Here one incident
shows that the symbolic values of the Lefferts Manor
will continue to play a role in reactions to newcomers, despite what outside observers might expect
to be the case. In the spring of 1971, a rumor was
spread in the Manor that a "hippie commune" was being
set up in one of the houses on Midwood Street. The
hippies were brownstoners. Those who heard the rumor
spoke of the drug problems and wild parties that were
certain to materialize in the community. A few months
after the rumor was started, it was discovered that
the "commune" was merely a young white couple who
had recently moved into a large brick brownstone.
The "hippiness" was hypothesized by local common-
sense sociologists from the appearance of the husband--
long hair and mustache--and the motorcycle that was
parked outside the door. He and his wife both wore
patched blue jeans, and occasionally walked around,
barefoot, on the sidewalk. They were also overheard
employing various obscenities in ordinary conversation. The "commune" suspicion was raised because a
few friends had stayed over in the house for a few
days to help the newcomers settle in.

The Invasion Mentality

How has the Lefferts Manor and the larger neighborhood around it responded to numerous invasions? Most of the reaction, in defense of their particular definitions of the community--that of middle-class propriety--has been the tendency to isolate the invaders from the established community. When they are convinced that the newcomers share the same, or similar, community values, the isolation gradually lessens. The Lefferts Manor Association, an organization of one-family homeowners who cling to the exclusive traditions of their community, is a bureaucratic expression of these communal values. The reluctance of churches to admit newcomers is a similar phenomenon. The practice of exclusion and then reluctantly accepting invaders into churches has severely weakened the power of local religious institutions. Discrimination undermines their viability and membership rolls decline over the years, leaving many of them more architectural reminders of what were once very important local centers of social life. Only during the last decade, since 1970, have a few churches revitalized their roles in the community by involvement in nonsectarian activities such as day care, cultural and social services.

For the most part, major negative reactions to change in the neighborhood have been individual and collective and not truly associational (except for the Lefferts Manor Association's defense of the covenant). Not all of the activities of Manorites have been negative in orientation. Some, with greater economic and psychic investment in their community have made major commitments to promote their community positively by seeking publicity which highlights the positive qualities of the neighborhood and have even come together with "outsiders" in joint community ventures. These activists are attempting, in a way that is new for Manorites, to defend their community and the definitions of it which are under constant attack by people who hold biased assumptions about the possible quality of life in black and integrated areas.

Although many of the incidents depicted in the foregoing pages, and others like them which will be presented in following ones, can easily be interpreted as bigotry and the generally negative side of human nature, they should be considered more

carefully. In the case of the Lefferts Manor they
should be seen as products of mechanisms for defending the viability and stability of the community. To
use Gerald Suttles's terms, the Manor is a "defended"
and not a "defeated" community.[7] These actions
demonstrate that despite the many changes in the
area, Manorites continue to feel that their community
is a sacred and exalted place, and that they expect
others to respect that image.

The hostile reaction of Manorites to invaders
may be regarded by some liberal thinkers as residues
of regressive village mentalities which are out of
place in the modern urban world. However, with the
growing concern for neighborhood and city preservation, and rehabilitation of decayed central cities,
the desire of local people to protect their homes
and their ways of life should not be targeted for
elimination. Even racial discrimination obscures
more basic, positive feelings about community life
in the city. Neighborhoods should not be destroyed
either physically or symbolically. Up until this
time we have paid most of our attention in the
fields of urbanology to the physical aspects of
cities. Perhaps we can gain some needed insight
into urban problems through a new perspective which
emphasizes the symbolic aspects of urban life.

It is when people react passively, or actively
to destroy their homes and neighborhoods, when their
communities are invaded that the city has most to
fear. If valuable meanings of neighborhoods are lost
or defiled, all that is left is the economic value of
inner-city property which is to be disposed of or
exploited rather than to be treasured and passed on
to deserving heirs. When the destruction of positive
neighborhood images in the central cities, and in the
suburbs as well, occurs, these communities are likely
to become afflicted by the diseases that ultimately
lead to urban decay.

Despite all the hostility vented toward invading
groups, prejudice, discrimination, racism, anti-
Semitism, and parochialism, the Lefferts Manor has a
chance to remain a respectable, middle-class community
in the middle of what might become a sea of low-income
ghettoes. There, people will sweep the sidewalks and
observe the mannerisms of community togetherness. For
the most part Manorites share one important thing in
common--they define their streets, homes, life-styles

118

and themselves as worth defending, not only
physically but symbolically as well.

Chapter V

MICROLOGICAL ASPECTS OF URBAN PROBLEMS

No matter how hard the residents of the Lefferts Manor tried to keep their community from ever changing, they could not succeed in that impossible task. All neighborhoods change and develop. Change can be slowed or accelerated, but never completely stopped. Trying to control social change, at the grass roots level, is an almost futile endeavor. Neighborhoods that depend on segregation and closure for their survival are bound to be destroyed. The Manor was not an exceptional community because it never changed, but because the modifications there came about more slowly, and more gracefully, than in nearby areas.

Involuntary Change: Aging and Death

The original residents of the Lefferts Manor are all but extinct. When they passed away, their homes became part of family estates; the houses and contents being sold or inherited by, in most cases, distant heirs. One pair of newcomers to the Manor in 1973, purchased a house which was previously owned by two unmarried elderly women. While rummaging through the house, the newcomers became a team of amateur archaeologists, discovering indictions of a past civilization. The artifacts they uncovered gave them some insight into the life-styles of early Manor Brahmins. They found symbols of affluence and opulence--silver serving pieces, a luxurious dining area and many very formal pieces of furniture, and artwork. They hypothesized that the household included a number of servants, because of an extensive bell system which connected living areas with work areas of the house. Also, among the archaeological evidence were diaries, newspaper clippings and letters which, upon reading, conveyed to them the impression that the owners were of high social standing. And in one room, they found the personal effects of a brother who was a nineteenth-century captain of a merchant ship.

The history of the family who lived in this three-story brownstone also shows how some of the residential succession in the Manor took place. It seems that many of the earliest residents of the Manor moved away, but retained their homes in the community as town houses as the community underwent various transitions. In many instances the propensity of white upper-middle-class urbanites, who were once in the majority, to have limited progeny eventually led to their disappearance not only from the Manor, but from the human community as well. The two spinsters and their bachelor brother who lived here left no heirs. The sisters died, alone, in the house. They also had no close relations, and the home passed in probate to a distant nephew.

The fading away of the original Manorites might be partially illuminated by these bits of local history gleaned from the pages of the Manor Association's <u>Manor Echo</u>.

> One family which is to be ranked among the very early residents of the Manor is the Cox family, now represented by <u>Miss</u> Eileen Cox and her aunt, Kathleen McMurray.
> Among the first "settlers" in the Midwood block between Rogers and Bedford was Jere J. Conran and his wife Mary V. Conran. It is interesting to learn that the <u>only remaining member</u> of the family, Virginia Cheasty (Mrs. John C. Cheasty), still resides at 196 Midwood Street to which her mother moved as a bride. . . . She says there were <u>relatively few children</u> in the Manor during the early part of the century. . . .
> Mr. Lawrence J. McSherry of 28 Maple St. has an estate on Long Island but retains this home as his town house. . . . He remembers when much of Maple St. between Flatbush and Bedford consisted of vacant lots. (January 1969)

The early Manorites remaining in the community are rare, and very old, but still play an important social role in the area. Long-term residents are, so to speak, the living social conscience and memory of the community. One old lady, for years before she died, sat outside her home every afternoon under the watchful eye of her black nurse-companion. She had

been nearly blind for many years. Despite her lack
of sight, she would chat with neighbors who passed
by about "seeing" the neighborhood going downhill.
The cause of the decline, she said, were the black
newcomers, to whom she referred as the "element."

The "element," or similar code word, has been
used in the past and present to stand for Jews,
Catholics, Italians and others who were seen as
threatening the Manor by their proximity to, or
residence in, the community. In the early 1970s,
the "element" was the founders of the Prospect-
Lefferts-Gardens Neighborhood Association which
promoted racial integration, and tried to service
the lower-class people in the area through community
programs. These people were viewed as a threat
because they highlighted the problems that defile
the sacred character of the Lefferts Manor.

There is some irony in the perceptions of
older residents as to the causes of the neighborhood
decline. In many cases it is their homes, particularly the property of oldsters with no family and
limited income, that are in the worst physical
condition. Not having younger family members to
care for them, or their homes, and being extremely
security conscious (so much so that they do not
invest in repairs and maintenance), their once
beautiful exteriors fall into disrepair; front
yards are over-grown and littered: broken windows
and peeling paint are highly visible features of
the poorer senior citizens' homes. The newest
invaders to the Manor, when they buy homes from
these estates, are faced with extensive repairs due
to the long years of neglect and abuse of the property. For example, the young "archaeologists"
mentioned earlier, related that they had a great
deal of trouble removing urine stains from their
parquet floors. Other couples interviewed told of
even more indelicate hygienic situations in rooms
of houses they had purchased. One local resident
said that he knew of several instances of elderly
people dying in their homes, alone. In some cases
it was several days before neighbors investigated.
When the homes were entered by police or neighbors,
what they saw was shockingly depressing: human
waste and food garbage strewn on the floors, gaping
holes in ceilings due to leaks that were never
repaired--a horror of filth and disarray. The
causes of these disgraceful scenarios are quite

simple: age, disability, fear, loneliness, and poverty. In many places the poorer abandoned aged confine themselves to one or two rooms of their huge homes for the many years prior to their passing.

Within a community all individual parts are interconnected to form a comprehensive whole. Therefore, the problems of the disadvantaged elderly are a problem for the Manor. Since they cannot care for themselves, they cannot help to maintain the image of the community. Fortunately for the Manor, the proportion of elderly experiencing economic hardship is small. Although this segment of the population has given up the defense of the special image of the community, and their own image as well, their participation in the degradation of the community has been for the most involuntary.

Some of the other older residents have found that living alone is unbearable and so some form what might be called old people's communes. Brothers, sisters, close relatives and old friends come together in order to share the burdens of their twilight years. It is not unusual to see, during the day, old people assisting one another as they try to follow patterns of everyday life that they have established over the many years spent in the Manor. Even walking a city block to get to a grocery store, however, becomes a major chore, and some do not venture outside their homes for these short excursions. They have all their provisions delivered to them at home. The presence of elderly people, and the many more in nearby apartment houses, makes security a primary concern of both old and young Manorites. Old people in city neighborhoods attract crime like a magnet because they are such easy targets.

It is not difficult to imagine the intense fear that grips the elderly as they walk the streets. They are presented with so many unfamiliar faces, and to an old person, a young black or brown face is a symbolic threat to their safety. At night the elderly lock themselves behind strong doors and occasionally peer out between the bars on windows. Stronger bars, locks and alarm systems are often the only improvements they have made on their homes in recent years. These people are not merely reacting to the actual crime rate in the Manor, which, although high, is much lower than in other nearby areas, but to the "signs" of urban crime. They also react to media reports of city and national crime waves. To the aged even the Manor can become the proverbial "jungle" of the modern urban world.

Besides the actual crimes against the elderly which take place, even the smallest incident is spread among the oldtimers and in the process is inflated to major proportions; pocketbook snatching becomes robbery and assault. Crimes that take place blocks away are believed to have taken place around the corner. Reactions to crime and crime reports are bound to be exaggerated due to inefficient communication networks and the pervasiveness of fear. To the aged some "element" is always responsible for crime and other social problems in the Manor. Unable to flee, they retreat further and further into their mental worlds and the neighborhood for them becomes, what Joseph P. Lyford called an "Airtight Cage" (1966).

The most important need for the viability of a human community, which is after all a biological unit, is generational succession. As a social community, generation succession is also the passing of traditions from the old to the young, regardless of the existence of biological connections between them. It can be argued that for older Manor residents, their community will pass with them into oblivion. They themselves, however, are history and tradition, and they will always have an impact on those who come to the Lefferts Manor after them. From the first to the last, Manorites are eternally and historically fused. By their constant negative remarks on the changes in the community and by their overt discrimination over the years, the oldtimers will always be remembered by newcomers. The Lefferts Manor has a long history of making people feel unwanted, undesirable and unworthy of receiving its sacred grace. Perhaps that is part of the reason why it still is such a "good" neighborhood today.

Attitudes of Heirs

There are many other people who are much more dangerous to the Manor because they are either ignorant of the symbolic value of the community, or hold other values that they consider to be more important. For example, it is not unusual for the property of deceased or institutionalized oldtimers to be taken

124

over by persons who are not familiar with the area.
These people often consider the property to be an
economic liability because it is the "inner city."
A few have abandoned their inherited houses, but more
sell them for low prices to real estate speculators
who try to convert the structure to multiple-family
or rooming house uses.

Since 1960, the attempts by heirs and agents to
convert Manor property to commercial use seems to be
related to the perception of the community by outsiders that, because the population is predominately
nonwhite, there would be little chance of finding
buyers of one-family homes. The Manor to these
people is "just another place," not a unique, elite
community which deserves special treatment. White
and nonwhite homeowners reported that they found it
difficult to find Manor homes on the open real estate
market. When they learned of a Manor house for sale,
black buyers in particular were told by agents and
lawyers that they would have little difficulty finding
renters or roomers, who would make it easier to pay
mortgage and other costs.

Even after black Manorites moved in they were
often referred to by deliverymen and others as
"tenants." Their mail slots were stuffed with
letters and flyers addressed to numerous "occupants."
Today this is a more common non-racial phenomenon.
These and other occurrences make it quite clear that
the one-family definition of the Lefferts Manor is
not universally shared. It is also clear that the
ignorance of this special meaning, or disrespect for
it, presents a constant danger to the viability and
stability of the community.

Apartment Houses: The Big Change

The construction of large apartment houses near
the Lefferts Manor eliminated the flat, suburban
landscape of Flatbush and symbolically polluted the
elite residential community. Most of the buildings,
erected in the 1920s, were intended to be luxury
apartment houses. The objective advantages of the
area insured that even high-density residential
developments would initially be occupied by high
status intruders. Over the next forty years, however,
the social status of new and old tenants was to slowly
decline.

125

Two major factors were instrumental in this process of decline. The first was aging. By the time the wealthiest tenants of the luxury apartments were passing away or retiring to their suburban estates, the Prospect-Lefferts-Gardens area was no longer the kind of neighborhood that "modern" rich people thought of as a "proper" setting for themselves. Therefore, they were replaced by more ordinary kinds of individuals and families. Also, as the years passed many of the upper-middle-class and middle-class tenants became part of the growing population of urban aged poor. These people, who once held well-paying and important positions in private and public affairs slipped into semi-poverty upon retirement. They also were more likely than the independently wealthy to be induced to remain in the area as it changed because of the vagaries of New York City rent laws which for a long time froze their rents at pre-1950 rates.

The second factor was the loss of the incentive for landlords to maintain luxury apartment buildings. At the same time the city was losing prospective tenants to the suburbs, wage increase demands of labor, soaring inflation and utility rates, and other more attractive investment opportunities made the old-fashioned landlord an endangered species. Increasingly, apartment houses were acquired by large anonymous rental management corporations. At the same time that costs were rising, government-imposed controls on rents limited the prices landlords could ask for their apartments. The scarcity of apartments after the Second World War, and the high incidence of rent "gouging" at the time led to public pressure for controls. The "emergency" controls were to last as long as the city-wide vacancy rate was low. Rapidly escalating construction costs, increased difficulty in obtaining loans for new construction, and the spiraling rate of apartment house abandonment insured that the vacancy rate would remain too low for the lifting of restrictions. There have been several revisions, and additions, to the original rent laws but none of them have decreased the unprofitability of maintaining older buildings.

In general, the rent laws, economic downturns and the demographic transition within the city have created a situation in which landlords cannot find it profitable to improve, or even maintain their older

properties. They find it advantageous on the other
hand to create and maintain high apartment turnover
rates because each turnover allows for a legal rent
increase. It is obvious that, under these conditions,
residential succession in older buildings would result
in newcomers being of lower social standing than the
older tenants--Who else would pay more money for
fewer services?

Although all the complexities of renting and
building apartments in the city are beyond the scope
of this volume, one other interesting factor in the
social change of Brooklyn apartment houses must be
noted.[1] During the 1960s, with large numbers of
landlords searching for better sources of income
for their deteriorating units, the Department of
Social Services began having difficulty finding
dwelling places for its increasing client population
of indigent nonwhite families. Abandonment, arson
and demolition of units in low-income neighborhoods
led the Department to look more and more into
middle-class areas for vacancies. This was also
the period of government attention and intervention
in the racial segregation patterns in New York City.
In order to overcome the reluctance of people to
rent to welfare families, the Department offered
to pay higher rents to landlords--in many cases far
above rent-controlled ceilings. Another inducement
were "finders fees" for providing suitable apartments. Some landlords jumped at these opportunities
and "packed" their buildings with as many welfare
families as they could.

The mere presence of a few welfare, usually
nonwhite, families in a white, middle-class building
was sufficient to raise rents in a round-about way.
The invasion of poor residents caused many long-time
tenants to move out, thus allowing the landlord to
raise the rent for those apartments. In essence the
Department of Social Services engaged in well-
intentioned "block busting," which has since
decreased. The elimination of inducements has to
some degree moderated the panic flight of middle-
class whites from some Brooklyn, high-density
neighborhoods.

The unholy alliance between city departments,
civil rights organizations and some landlords had
other, less predictable effects on apartment buildings
and neighborhoods. Not only did the alliance result

127

in increased profits for landlords, they were also provided with relatively docile tenants who viewed their residences as "temporary" quarters. Welfare families are frequently relocated, and seldom stay in a community long enough to develop a sense of belonging. Also, the reactions of other residents to them further reduces their interest in becoming active members of the community. These problems are in addition to their socio-economic and cultural disadvantages. Landlords, then, were able to take adventage of these tenants to an even greater degree than they had of older tenants. Poor tenants, unaware of their rights and lacking incentive to fight for them, were treated to increasingly deteriorated facilities and decreasing services.

It was not until the mid-1960s that problems in the financing and operations of multiple dwellings led to the steadily more rapid influx of non-elite, and then poor, tenants into apartments near the Lefferts Manor. It is easy to imagine the hostility, and conflicts that ensued between older and newer tenants, and the growing fears of Manorites, some of whom lived only across the street from declining buildings. Manor residents always had regarded tenants as intruders in the neighborhood, even when the tenants were of relatively high social standing. When the buildings began losing their upper-class residents, the social and psychological distances between Manorites and their unwanted neighbors increased proportional to their lower-class status. The conflict and competition between tenants and homeowners is "natural" in that each group sees their interests as being in opposition to the other.

Most Manorites believe that apartment houses, and tenants are "problems" per se. Their solution is to get rid of "them." Tenants often complain of the proprietory attitudes of Manor residents toward public streets and sidewalks. Manorites who live across from apartment buildings are even more likely than others not to recognize tenants as legitimate members of their community. Propinquity, in this case, does not lead to the extension of the social boundaries of community, but rather to their contraction. In the urban environment, the physical proximity of people to one another does not insure that they will share other things in common. What is necessary for the growth and maintenance of a neighborhood community is the sharing by people of a more comprehensive set of values and norms--things that do not ordinarily arise from the mere co-presence of neighbors.

Today, with the racial differences between Manorites and tenants disappearing, homeowners still for the most part refuse to participate with "them" in block association activities and other actions within the wider community. Most Manorites will not contribute their time, money, expertise or influence to help solve the problems of tenants, even though in many cases the solution of these problems would be beneficial to the Lefferts Manor. We might say that the attitude of Manorites is "irrational." Regardless of an objective appraisal of the situation, Manor residents feel that they have little in common with renters.

The Life of a Tenant and a Building

The following pages offer a biographical sketch of a tenant in what once was a luxury building near the Lefferts Manor. It may help us to understand both the relationship between tenants and homeowners in the neighborhood, and more importantly, how buildings and the people who live within them undergo transition. Ruth and her family moved into their five-room apartment on the western edge of Prospect-Lefferts-Gardens in 1945. Her husband had recently returned from active duty overseas during the Second World War, and had obtained a good job with a large accounting firm in Manhattan. They both thought that they had found the perfect neighborhood in which to raise their small family. Ruth recalled that during the first few years in the building, the owner seemed to "take great pride" in maintaining his property. He and his family lived in a large apartment on the top floor. The building's janitor also occupied an apartment in the buildings, and was easily accessible to the tenants. At that time, there were also uniformed elevator men, doormen, and other specialized building service employees who catered to the needs of the tenants.

The tenants, especially the older ones, were wealthy. Half of the residents were Jewish; the other half Gentile. All were white. The Gentiles were mostly middle-aged, or older, and were living in large six and seven room apartments even though

their children had grown and had moved away and the
space was not needed. Ruth said that these tenants
were " . . . well off. The women in the building would
go out shopping wearing white gloves, and hats."
Mothers were not allowed to stand outside in front of
the building with their baby carriages, and "hanging
around" near the entrance was frowned upon by the
manager--"It didn't look good." The tenants' children
were permitted to play only in the rear of the
property where there was a grassy play-area. "In front
of the building there were plants and gardens, and a
sculptured water fountain, that worked!" The entrance
to the building was covered by a glass canopy and
there was a circular drive for cars which was
landscaped in the center. In the middle of the
ground floor, there was a small courtyard where
people could sit and talk.

Of the seventy-five families in the building,
only four or five had small children when Ruth moved
in. "Most of the tenants thought that small children
were a nuisance and complained about them. Most of
the younger tenants were Jewish." This age, and
family-status division between Gentile and Jewish
tenants also engendered a number of anti-Semitic
remarks from the older, more established residents
who were not fond of children. Despite the problem
of "feeling out of place," Ruth liked the neighborhood
for many reasons. Transportation was excellent; the
subway ran directly to Manhattan where her husband
worked, and ran in the other direction to the beach.
She also remembered that the park nearby was a great
place for boating and picnicking. It was a "family"
park, and she "no fear of going into the park then."
She would walk to the park pushing her baby carriage
and meet with a group of mothers there and talk,
while the children played together. "When the
children grew older the area was good because it
was close to the library and the museum." They would
attend Sunday afternoon concerts there. "The area
was good for shopping too."

As the years went by, and the children grew
older, Ruth began to notice the animosity between
tenants and nearby homeowners. "The homeowners used
to chase the kids away from the block. They felt,
"How dare the children ride a bike and play ball;
even in the public streets. The homeowners considered
the street, a private street and the apartment people
did not. I told one that they did not own the street

nd that the kids could play there." Homeowners would
call the police when children played "stickball" (an
urban street game with rubber ball and broomstick
handle) in front of their houses. Once a policeman
came to Ruth's apartment to tell her that a complaint
had been made against her son for disturbing the
peace of the community. She was extremely indignant
and angry at the homeowner who had signed the
complaint. She thought her son was "very quiet." She
also thought that the homeowners were "sick" and hated
kids. For example, "One of the homeowners had
political influence and had a kid arrested for using
abusive language and threatening a homeowner,
alleged." When this occurred, in 1955, the parents
from the apartment building got together and pro-
tested at the police station to have the boy
released. "But he got a J.D. [juvenile delinquency]
card."

The longer Ruth and her family stayed in the
building, the more the high status Gentiles without
children moved or died. Middle-class Jewish families
replaced them, and gradually the building became popu-
ated with "average" younger families. Concomitant
with the loss of elites, Ruth noticed, the building
and surrounding area became less luxurious. The
building then passed into the hands of the owner's
son, who promptly became an absentee landlord by
moving to a Long Island suburb. The place was no
longer good enough for him. "The superintendent and
his family were moved into a basement apartment. . . .
and the back, where the children used to play, was
cemented over. So was the garden. There were no
repairs made in the building. The Persian rug in the
lobby was removed. The toilet seats were not
replaced when they wore out, as they used to be.
The landlord's agent said that the people had to pay
for them themselves, and the hallways that used to
be washed once or twice a week, were not cleaned at
all. The light bulbs in the halls were reduced
from sixty to fifteen watts. Then the landlord
demanded rent increases!"

Apartments were not painted for years, and the
tenants were harassed by agents when they complained
about the loss of services and the deterioration of
the building. "This led to more and more people
moving out." Once Ruth went to court with some other
tenants to argue that since the landlord had decreased
services over the years, that he was not entitled to

rent increases under the terms of the rent control law. To "prove" their claims, the tenants "before" and "after" photographs of the building. A rear and side entrance to the byilding had been closed. The landlord had continued to charge higher rents for "furnished" apartments even though he no longer furnished them. At one time there were washing machines and dryers in the basement which were used by servants, and in Ruth's time by the tenants themselves. Now the laundry room was gone. The expensive paintings that once graced the walls, and the expensive floor coverings were all missing from the building. The intercom and bell system no longer operated properly. Gone were the doormen stationed in front of the lobby to greet tenants and provide security.

The tenants won their case in court, but in the longer run they lost their battle with the landlord. The building continued to deteriorate as the owner argued that he could not afford to maintain it. As the building began its decline, Ruth noticed that the neighborhood also began to "change." "The streets got dirtier and more dangerous." People did not sweep their sidewalks anymore, and there were increased reports of street crimes and burglaries.

When Ruth's children were in public schools in the area, the schools had excellent reputations, and they were virtually all-white. New York, despite its "liberal" image has always had de facto racially segregated schools because of the use of a "neighborhood school" concept in planning. Neighborhoods were segregated; therefore schools were as well. Suddenly, in the late 1950s and early 1960s, racial integration of public schools became the cause celebre of the city's liberal politicians, and experiments in eliminating the segregation were begun. This caused panic in many white communities, and accelerated racial turnover in white areas that bordered black ones.

Eventually, black pupils entered public schools in Prospect-Lefferts-Gardens in large numbers. Black families moved into apartments and homes in the community as white families left. It must be noted here that frequently the "white flight" we hear so much about begins, not when blacks move into white residential areas, but before that--when black children come into local classrooms. The affluent

liberal or conservative sends his children to private
schools and when the neighborhood changes, moves. The
non-affluent white, liberal or conservative tries to
keep black children out of "their" schools and, failing
in that battle, also moves to a "whiter" neighborhood.

The Prospect-Lefferts-Gardens neighborhood
"changed," and so Ruth and many of her neighbors began
moving to other areas southward in Brooklyn, or out of
the Borough. This out-migration of white middle-class
apartment dwellers took on "flight" proportions in
the middle 1960s. The remnants of Ruth's cohort today
are the older Jewish and Gentile couples or
individuals who continue to resent and fear their
"new" neighbors. In the white communities of southern
Brooklyn, those that fled Central Brooklyn areas are
today fighting against racial integration of their
schools and neighborhoods, as are suburban ex-
Brooklynites.

Neighborhood leaders in southern Brooklyn
white neighborhoods who are now faced with problems
of integration often say that "this has happened to
them before." A sort of sociological deja vu!
Although it is difficult to feel sympathy toward
people who are literally bigoted, the sociologist must
understand that they have suffered greatly because of
their own irrationality. Their prejudices have been
so well exploited by others who have profited enor-
mously from their fear of nonwhites. Incompetent
white politicians continue to be elected by whispering
to their constituents that, if elected, they will keep
"them" out. Nonwhite politicians see white flight as
the opening of new territory. One real estate agent,
who "works" the Brooklyn areas I have studied,
casually noted that he and his agency have in many
instances bought and sold the homes of local people
several times; first in northern Brooklyn, second in
Central Brooklyn and now the third home in southern
Brooklyn. And each time the agent makes a profit.
Racial prejudice has been the foundation of lucrative
real estate enterprises in many American cities. I
should emphasize that the black real estate agents
and brokers are no less willing to take advantage of
racial fears, and the limited availability of decent
housing for blacks. This situation allows for the
appearance of cooperative black-white relations--in
real estate.

Understanding Intricate Urban Problems

We can be sure that all Manorites have been
exposed to some Lefferts Manor propaganda. Knowledge and appreciation of the positive definitions of
the community is the cornerstone of its viability.
But, just as positive definitions of community help
to preserve it, negative or neutral ones can lead to
its accidental or purposeful destruction. Negative
and neutral ideas about the Lefferts Manor emanate
from many sources, inside and outside of the
community. Let us now consider some of these sources,
the activities they generate and their resultants
which undermine the high value placed on the area.

On one street there are many violations of the
Manor's one-family only covenant. Here multi-family
and single-room-occupancy dwellings, owned by absentee
landlords, have taken over a number of ten- and
twelve-room Victorian row houses. An informant on
the block alleged that one of the buildings is a
veritable "hotel" for West Indian immigrants. Illegal
tenants stay for a few weeks as they seek more permanent residences, and employment. Although violations
are an "open secret,"[2] little has been done about the
problem. One neighbor was very upset by the "shameful
situation" but was afraid of reprisals if she openly
complained, and signing a complaint against the owner
would remove any possibility of anonymity. Others
have expressed similar reservations, but the most
common excuse for inaction is that some "higher
authority" should do something about the problem
and not ordinary citizens.

This attitude toward local problems is typical
in communities of "limited liability," where power
is vested in central, supra-community authorities.[3]
Over the years, even special communities like the
Manor have been alienated from the sources of
political power in the city. Authorities answer
criticism of their inertia by complaining that they
cannot do anything of great value without verified
citizen complaints, and the willingness of neighbors
to sue other neighbors in court. In effect, their
inaction creates a stalemate in the community in
which people tolerate all but the most obnoxious
of violations.

Multiple-family use of Manor homes creates
other problems, concrete and symbolic. Many

defenders of the covenant are themselves violating the letter of the law. Aging brothers and sisters, as well as other more distant relatives often share houses, segregating themselves by floors or rooms. This is easy to accomplish because Manor homes are so large. Some of the "respectable" deviants go so far as to "actually" violate the covenant by installing an extra kitchen, thereby establishing, officially, the existence of separate households. Most modifications are also obtained without obtaining the mandated city variances and construction permits. As long as the "front" of the building, and other "public" aspects of the building are maintained in a single-family style, neighbors simply look the other way.

It is the "virtual" examples of norm violation that are most likely to cause consternation among Manorites, but not the "actual" deviance itself.[4] If someone ran a rooming house in which all tenants shared a "family resemblance," and were circumspect about the other rules of the Lefferts Manor social code, no one would be the wiser. Even if neighbors were "wise" to the situation, it would be ignored. This brings to mind a problem of racial perceptions in the area. Given the general inability of whites and nonwhites to recognize each other's physical idiosyncracies, Manorites of different ethno-racial backgrounds are more likely to see their counterparts as family members--"they all look alike." In America we generally hear about this problem of perceptual bias as being one exclusively of whites vis-a-vis nonwhites. But, in doing this research, and interviewing people from a wide range of ethno-racial backgrounds, it became clear that "everyone looks alike." For example, one black man, whom I had interviewed and had worked with on several community projects, still mistakes me for another white person. I have brown hair, blue eyes and am generally clean shaven. My Doppleganger is two inches taller, has black hair, brown eyes and sports a bushy beard that covers most of his face.

This recognition problem can make people feel uneasy in many social situations. Often people do not know that their neighbors, with whom they are "friendly," are not related to one another. Three young black-haired white women on one block are constantly taken for each other by nonwhites, even though they have lived there for over four years.

135

Blacks are differentiated by whites via "light skinned" versus "dark skinned" recognition criteria. Respectively, whites are "fat" or "skinny." If we turn to the proper recognition of children, we find even less visual differentiation. In the community there are "black kids" and "white kids." Given these perceptual problems in heterogeneous neighborhoods, it is no wonder that groups, and not individuals, are blamed for local problems. "Collective guilt" is at least partially due to recognition difficulties.

How would an "outsider" know of a one-family covenant violation? Authorities claim that they cannot act without specific signed complaints, and then an inside inspection of the dwelling unit. Legally they cannot perform the inspection without the permission of the owner, because the house is certified as a one-family building. This puts city authorities in a "Catch-22" dilemma.

There are other scientifically valid but not legally useful methods of finding violations. One is the "ask the mailman" procedure. Variants of this technique are the "ask the gasman, deliveryboy, etc." techniques. All these people are similarly endowed with access to the inside of buildings--Goffman's "backstage."[5] The mailman delivers letters and packages which may be addressed to many different family names. Gas and electric meter readers regularly enter homes, and in particular, have the best view of basements that have been converted to apartments, which are in violation of both health and building codes.

More sophisticated, but still relatively simple, means of investigation focus on the use of public and private utilities. Higher than expected gas, water and electric consumption can give clues to excess occupancy. The counting of independent telephone hook-ups on outside poles, or using a reverse telephone directory which lists phone customers by address, can also be helpful in zeroing in on violations.

Violation of the one-family covenant is not merely a symbolic problem. Manorites pay higher real estate taxes for the privilege of the non-commercial protection. Public services to the area are based on official population estimates and projections of need. For example, Manorites have

136

heir garbage collected on a schedule based on
xpectation of volume produced by low-density one-
amily areas. The "invisible" residents produce
isible refuse which slows down the collection
rocess, and leads to the overflowing of garbage
nto Manor streets and sidewalks. The stench of
otten garbage is hardly a pleasant experience, but
t is even worse for those who have sought refuge in
ne Manor from more odoriferous neighborhoods.

Police protection for the neighborhood is
lso planned on the basis of expectations of the
mount of crime usually transpiring in single-
amily community. One-family areas are generally
ow-crime areas; therefore the Manor is under-
atrolled. School construction and educational
rograms and budgets are planned using estimates
f population size, age cohorts, density of the area
nd types of local households. The invisible popu-
ation in the community then results in overcrowding
t local public schools, and further decreases the
illingness of middle-class people to send their
nildren to neighborhood schools, insuring the
redominance there of low-income minority children.

The quality of telephone service to the Manor
s diminished because of illegal occupancy as old
elephone wires are tapped into beyond their capacity.
nis leads to overloads of calls, busy signals at
eak hours, and frequent mechanical breakdowns of
ncient equipment. Water supply, gas and electricity
re, in a sense, the life sustaining fluids of urban
ommunities. In areas where there are large numbers
f uncounted people, the energy and water supplies
hat are pumped into the community are generally
nsufficient for local demand. In reference to
ocal water supply, the conduits which carry it
ere designed for less volume. Over-demand
ecreases the flow and pressure in pipes, and this
esults in brown, rusty and often unpotable liquid.
ain breaks occur more frequently, and residential
treets are torn apart to make repairs. Fire
rotection is diminished as hydrants offer up
nsufficient amounts to suffocate local blazes.
inally, taking a shower in an illegal three-or-
ore-family house can be dangerous, if someone
ecides to flush the toilet at the time you are
n the shower stall.

Excess population overtaxes the electric grids
that run under city streets. "Blackouts"--complete
loss of electric service--can result from these overloads. More often local "brownouts" take place--a
reduction in current which can dim lights and overtax
electric appliances. The most dangerous times in
recent years for outages have been the summer months
when air conditioners are in use, especially in the
early evening hours when large numbers of people
come home from work and switch on their cooling units.

Least dramatic, but most frustrating, of the
problems caused by excess population is over-popula-
tion of local automobiles, which increase at almost
the same rate as people. America is a car-dominated
society, and even urban dwellers who would do well
without a car feel "less than whole" without one.
Parking and traffic plans are based on area population
estimates. In over-populated neighborhoods problems
are a natural outcome of ignorance of actual numbers
of residents. Although Manor property lots vary in
size, the frontages are generally eighteen to twenty-
two feet in width. This space allows for the parking
of one American-sized car. The addition of a few
extra one- or two-car families on the block can
then, produce agony for Manorites who must search
the streets several blocks away from their house for
a safe place to park their cars. Even Manorites who
have garages or driveways are not immune to the
problem, as space-hungry drivers block their
driveways due to the shortage of legal anchorage.
The insult that is added to injury in the Manor
results from the neighborhood being treated by the
local police as a "favored" area. Patrolmen, and
other empowered city agents, ticket illegally parked
cars in the Manor with a vengeance due to the high
volume of complaints by influential or simply "loud"
residents about illegally parked cars.

In recent years, New York City has instituted
an "alternate side of the street" parking program,
in which every other day one side of the street is
off-limits to parked cars. This allows mechanical
street sweepers to clear the curbs of accumulated
debris, as New Yorkers have retreated from doing it
themselves. During half of the week, then, one-half
of the potential parking spaces in the neighborhood
are eliminated from eight to eleven o'clock in the
morning. The shrinking of the area for legal parking
increases the parameters of the parking space hunt

that takes place each evening and early morning.

Many Manorites receive on the average of one parking ticket every other month at fifteen dollars per infraction. It would cost more than fifteen to twenty dollars per month to park at a local parking lot, so taking a chance every day is more economical than avoiding the problem completely by renting a parking space. If one avoids being ticketed, one is not immune to anger at not having a safe place to park a car that is so heavily taxed by local government. Also, the exaggerated concern over parking in the Manor is related to the belief held by Manorites that they have "arrived." Most have celebrated the event by purchasing boat-sized automobiles, or second cars. One must only dwell upon the undignified appearance of a double-parked Cadillac to understand the Manorites' consternation.

Some of the threats to the symbolic value of the Manor are much more serious than others. Although two or three related families living together in a Lefferts Manor house may seem to an outsider as equivalent to the same number of unrelated families sharing the same quarters, Manorites do not see it that way. They believe that the latter situation is a threat to their individual and collective esteem. Neighbors will complain to authorities about loud illegal bottle clubs, prostitution and the sale or use of drugs by outsiders. They will also bemoan the loud noises and unkept backyards of illegal residents, but the loud parties, loose sexual practices, private drug use, noisy children, and the sloppiness of legitimate neighbors are all but ignored.

The hesitance of people to react vigorously to attacks on their symbolic territory is not difficult to understand. To complain loudly, openly and energetically is to make public one's collective and personal debasement. People like to keep their community skeletons in the closet. Most people shy away from calling attention to the negative aspects of their self-community. Those who have given up on the community are the most likely persons to be "public" complainers. Some few individuals also receive psychological gratification, a sort of self-flagellation, from exposing community sores. Those who have the greatest egoistic investments in the neighborhood, when they work to solve local problems,

do so quietly so as not to arouse publicity. In
respectable neighborhoods residents are generally
against demonstrations and picketing which to them
are synonomous with lower-class communities. In the
"better" areas these kinds of community actions are
taken only as a last resort.

Commercial vice problems create other kinds of
fears in the minds of neighborhood bystanders--such
as fear for personal safety. People are afraid to
openly complain, in expectation of retaliation by
criminal elements. Most city people have lost confidence in the ability of local law enforcement to
protect them from abuse. Logically, they argue that
if the police cannot prevent the primary offense, they
cannot deter the secondary crimes that could be
visited on complainants. Finally, and most effectively, past experience has taught many community
members that "nothing can be done," and this message
has been carried by the otherwise inefficient intra-
community communication network.

On Midwood Street, where the vast majority of
brownstones are still one-family, a group of concerned
people had tried unsuccessfully for several years to
have an after-hours bottle club closed on their
street. The club was located in a house that was
also an illegal multiple-family unit. The unfortunate
side-effect of their frustrating pursuit has been a
decrease in the willingness of neighbors to participate in problem-solving activities. After several
months of meetings and discussions of the problem
only a few diehards, who live nearest to the problem,
are left as activists. Those who live near the club
suggest, half-jokingly, that perhaps a bomb should
be thrown into the building, but this course of
action is still unrealistic for Manorites. Other
suggestions, such as the slicing of club patrons'
tires, or throwing bricks through their windows are
more realistic, but equally unlikely to be acted
upon. In the city most people are alienated from
both the legitimate and the illegitimate means of
social control.

Some community activists are certain that the
police at the local precinct are "paid off" by the
bottle club owners for protection. The regular,
almost decennial, reports of New York City Police
Department corruption add a great deal of popular
support for this theory. Such local suspicions add

o the collective lack of self-confidence in grass-
oots community action as a means of solving problems.
ne incident that took place just outside the Manor's
oundaries, on the other side of the tracks, is
nstructive as to vigilantism and confidence in local
olice protection for the community. There had been
 rash of burglaries and muggings on a street of
orking-class homeowners and tenants. The residents
ere certain that the perpetrators of the crimes
hung around" the corner at a local "dive." Block
ssociation pleas to the precinct brought no help.
he residents of the block, virtually all of whom
ere black, had at earlier times lived in black
eighborhoods which were racked with crime and
new of police inaction when it came to problems
n minority group neighborhoods.

The men from the block called a meeting and
ecided to "take the law into their own hands."
everal armed themselves with baseball bats and
ther truncheons, and marched en masse around the
lock to confront their antagonists and "teach them
 lesson." The besieged, alleged criminals ran
nto their bar home base and refused to come out
 face community summary justice. They phoned the
ocal precinct house and asked for help. The police
uickly responded to the call and saved them from
he wrath of the community. One of the men who
articipated noted that the arrival of the police
as the quickest he had ever seen. This incident
eems to point out that the lower the social
tatus of the community residents, the more likely
hey are to engage in vigilante actions, and that
uthorities, such as the police, in these communities
ct not as arms of the community but as mediators
etween elements within it.

In reference to problems with bottle clubs in
esidential neighborhoods, even when the police do
espond to calls from irate residents, they do little
ore than ask a few questions and then leave. When
ressed about their inaction, police officials respond
hat they are hampered by a lack of community coopera-
ion. If neighbors complain loudly and frequently
nough, the "community relations" officer will reply
hat he is "working on it." If community protest
ontinues, the precinct might reply that its "hands
e tied" by the Supreme Court and the Constitution.

141

The way that bottle clubs are operated makes it difficult to close them down. It is illegal to sell alcoholic beverages in a private home. Bottle clubs can only sell "set-ups" (mixers, etc.) for drinks, as they lack a liquor license. The local zoning ordinances, however, prohibit even these sales. The patron of the club buys a ticket for a "party" from a friend, co-worker or solicitor on the street. Patrons can also pay at the door, which is discouraged as it increases the possibility that unwanted people, like the police, will gain entrance. The ticket entitles the bearer to a set-up, refreshments such as pretzels and potato chips, and the privilege to listen to the invariably loud music that blasts inside semi-dark rooms, and to bask in moving colored lights. If an undercover policeman cannot buy a drink, a verifiable ticket to an "amusement," or otherwise find evidence of illegal activities on the premises, he can do no more than enjoy himself for a while and then leave. Perhaps he will give a warning to the proprietor about the loud noises.

Other versions of "clubs" are the "rent party" and the "mortgage party" which are not uncommon in more ordinary city neighborhoods. Historically, city people who have found themselves short of cash at the end of the month, have resorted to fund-raising parties to come up quickly with the needed rent. For the Lefferts Manor this sort of behavior is "out of character." Manorites feel that if you cannot afford to live in a Manor house, you should not be here.

It is difficult to convince one's self that you have "made it" in the world, when a few doors down from you a constant stream of semi-intoxicated people are disembarking from cars and cabs, creating a traffic jam of honking autos on your otherwise sedate block. The elite image of your community is even more difficult to maintain when the patrons of the club seek relief on a hot summer's night from the stale, smokey club air and spill out onto the street. The sacrilege occurs when the revelers relieve their bladders on the azalea bush that some Manorite planted last spring because it gave the home a dignified appearance.

An example of the peculiar views of Manorites toward the commercial use of Manor property is the

142

"selective inattention" they display toward the
residences of practicing doctors, dentists and other
professionals. Professionals often have offices in
their homes from which they conduct business, and
receive clients. They generally convert the ground
floor of their homes into offices and work space.
Extra bathrooms and kitchen facilities, with parti-
tions for separate quarters, are also installed.
This makes the floor into a self-contained unit--an
apartment. Although these modifications are violations of the covenant and zoning codes, they are all
but ignored by most Manorites--"After all, they are
professionals." If, however, a local entrepreneur
were to convert a floor, or basement, of a Manor
house for use as a day-care center, carpentry or
auto repair shop, the reaction of most Manorites
would be outrage. Different types of social and
economic activities have varying social meanings
attached to them.

Unfortunately, when professionals sell their
homes, it is very tempting to buyers to allow the
violations to remain intact, and to exploit them.
Often it is suggested to the buyer that the property
has a higher value because of the potential money-
making uses. Once a newcomer turned a large
dentist's office into a day-care center in the
Jefferts Manor. The residents on the block never
complained about the dental practice, but were
adamant about the removal of the center, which
they thought was a "danger to the block." One
doctor, who himself violated the covenant, complained
that he was thinking of selling his house on the
block because the day-care center would "ruin the
neighborhood." In all likelihood the doctor will
sell his house without reservation to another
opportunist. Once the street is defined by someone
as already destroyed symbolically, it becomes easier
for them to add another straw to the community's
growing burden.

A serious threat to any city neighborhood occurs
each time property is transferred. About four percent
of Manor homes are sold, or otherwise passed on to new
owners each year. Many first enter into estates that
become the focus of time-consuming settlements.
During that time the property lies dormant and may
slowly deteriorate because of lack of maintenance.
At each "closing" the one-family covenant stands as
the legal protector of the community, but alone it

143

stands little chance of guaranteeing the integrity of
the Lefferts Manor. Without collective moral backing,
no legal restriction can be effective. Two-family
homes sell for more than single-family ones. To some
buyers a multi-family home is a must. Often lawyers
for estates, interested in seeing that the property
is sold as quickly as possible, neglect to tell their
clients of the restrictions on use of property, as it
may reduce interest in the sale.

I was told that one Manor landlord receives
twenty-five dollars per week for each of the thirteen
furnished rooms that he rents (this was 1975 rent), a
gross of $16,900 per year. With operating expenses
of between $4,000 and $5,000, this works out to a
profit of about $10,000 per year on an initial
investment of perhaps $30,000. Initial investments
can be much lower, and if the owner decides not to
pay real estate taxes, and skips on a mortgage;
besides skimping on maintenance and utilities, profits
can reach astronomical proportions. In this particular building, the approximately twenty tenants share
one large, and one small kitchen, and one large and
one small bathroom. Some of the tenants share rooms
on a "shift" basis--one rental partner works from
eight to four during the day and the other from
twelve midnight to eight in the morning. Although
these illegal tenants are hardworking, quiet people
they do present a danger to the community--most
obvious are health and safety problems caused by
overcrowding. There are also no fire escapes on the
building--they would be visible, and are also
illegal. Less obvious dangers are the excessive use
of the building's interior structure and overloading
of electrical wiring which increases the chance of
fire.

Newcomers, who have taken over properties that
were once rooming houses, tell of the extensive damage
to the insides of homes and the great costs of making
the homes "livable" again. After only a few years of
over-use by large numbers of tenants, the interiors
of Manor homes can be reduced to the condition of
hovels. Exteriors of buildings take a longer period
of time to fall apart. Also, even Manor homes in
poor interior condition are generally structurally
sound due to their excellent construction. Landlords
try to "dump" their "goldmines" when the physical
condition of the interior is so bad that they no
longer can attract enough tenants to make "working

em" profitable. Property may be semi-abandoned,
one or two floors remain habitable, and therefore
ntable to hard-pressed minority group workers. The
ndlord tries to keep the property until the house
almost totally deteriorated. A few houses in
ospect-Lefferts-Gardens have been taken over by
e city for non-payment of taxes, but this is rare
cause homes classified as one-family do not pay
mmercial tax rates. The use of single-family homes
rooming houses in the Manor is rare, but the
oblem in nearby neighborhoods is sometimes acute.
e over-use of buildings is a danger to all neigh-
rhoods, elite or not.

The shortage of adequate housing, particularly
r nonwhites, in the city creates an enticing and
crative opportunity for enterprising landlords. An
ditional factor--the large number of illegal aliens
the city--further aggravates the problem. Some
ople estimate that there are one million undocu-
nted workers in New York City, the plurality of
ich live in Brooklyn. These people must lose
emselves in nonwhite neighborhoods, such as
ospect-Lefferts-Gardens, and become grateful
r any place in which to stay.

There are other threats to good neighborhoods,
th or without covenants and protective zoning. A
w years ago there were a number of sensational
ories written in newspapers about extensive corrup-
on in the Federal Housing Administration's program
r urban areas. Prospect-Lefferts-Gardens and the
nor has been affected by this nationwide real estate
ip-off." In the schemes, poor people were sold
teriorated homes in inner city neighborhoods with
e help of FHA loans, illegally obtained for them
real estate professionals, often in collusion
th FHA workers.

Basically the "racket" operated this way:
andoned property and homes in run-down areas were
llected by brokerage houses, who also engaged in
e illegitimate sales. The brokers falsified appli-
tions for FHA mortgages by simple methods such as
flating the value of the house and the ability of
e client to carry to the loan, and underestimating
rrying charges and utilities. Frequently,
hantom" renovations were listed as improvements
the property in order to justify higher appraisals.
suspecting, and uninformed buyers then took over

145

houses that they could not afford to maintain. Some
resorted to renting rooms or used the property in
other commercial ventures to meet expenses. Most
failed in their attempts to maintain ownership and
the property was re-abandoned. The broker did not
lose anything in this process, as he was paid off the
top by the FHA loan. The lending institution was paid
by insurance. The poor owner lost the downpayment,
closing costs, tax payments and a "home." The Federal
Government lost the loan money and inherited a piece
of unsalable property. As an aside, it must be noted
that often the property was re-used in repeats of the
fraudulent real estate scheme.

One house in the Lefferts Manor, on a very
respectable block, became a casualty of FHA incom-
petence. The mortgage went into default, and the
property passed into FHA receivership. The tree-
lined street had a new addition, a three-story
brownstone with galvanized iron sheets draped over
the windows and doors. Tacked over the front door
was a small sign which read in part: "FBI. Anyone
entering upon or defacting this property will be
subject to prosecution." The sign was white with
red lettering. Many residents of the block interpreted the sign as an indication of pending urban
blight. Several people were interested in buying
the building and maintaining it as a single-family
home. They knew that the house would be a "good buy."
They first contacted the New York City Housing and
Development Administration, who referred them to...
who referred them to . . . etc. After several months
of searching, the interested buyers located a suburban
finance company which held title to the property. The
company's representative was quite surprised that a
middle-class, white person would be interested in
buying the house. The corporation had included the
Manor home in a package of "ghetto" homes to be
renovated for low-income family occupation. He said
that he thought the building was located in
Brownsville-East New York--two blighted neighborhoods
that are miles away from the Lefferts Manor geographically, and further away economically, socially
and symbolically to those who would be knowledgeable
about the city. The one thing that the Manor shared
with those urban low-income ghettoes was that they
were both predominately black neighborhoods.

Chapter VI

STIGMA AND SELF-IMAGE IN THE INNER CITY*

Brooklyn, as so many other cities, is essentially a collection of residential neighborhoods resting upon larger economic, political and social substructures. The traditional emphasis by urban scientific investigation on the economic plight of urban areas has led us to forget that the survival of most cities depends as much upon the well-being of residential as well as the industrial and business communities of cities. Cities have always been places that people call "home"--sacred, exalted places that are impregnated by residents with primary, face-to-face meaningfulness.[1] Modernization and urbanization have, of course, resulted in what Max Weber termed the "rationalization" of the human environment, and its consequent "disenchantment."[2] Although cities might be less "human" and communal than they once were, the urbanites who live within them still strive, as did their primitive counterparts, to impart social meanings to what some may argue are barren urban concrete and asphalt marketplaces, and industrial centers. The purpose of this chapter is to provide a sociological paradigm for understanding the methods by which ordinary people come to individual and collective grips with living in negatively defined urban territories. For the people in the Lefferts Manor, one technique for establishing socio-moral worth has already been outlined, the resort to valued history and traditions. Such legacies, however, are not as easily available to most other urban neighborhood residents, and Manorites must also face the fact that their own venerable history is neither universally known, nor respected by all those familiar with it. Therefore, the personal arks of Manorites float dangerously upon a sea of physically and socially polluted waves.

Urbanologists are constantly searching for concepts that have both theoretical and practical

Parts of this chapter have appeared in the Journal of Sociology and Social Welfare, The Humanist Sociologist and Brooklyn U.S.A.

value for the study of the city, and the generation of positive social polcies. One sociological concept, which has great potential utility for research and practice in negatively defined urban areas is Erving Goffman's "Stigma." He notes that:

> The Greeks, who were apparently strong on visual aids, originated the term "stigma" to refer to bodily signs designed to expose something unusual and bad about the moral status of the signifier. . . . Today the term is widely used in something like the original sense, but is applied more to the disgrace itself than the bodily evidence of it. (1963:1-2)

A stigma is, then, a negative aspect of personal identity. Although stigmatizing slaves, criminals or traitors through disfigurement--cutting or burning their flesh--might have its ancient roots in the Aegean Islands, there is enough of an Anglo-American tradition of branding deviants and human property for us to realize that stigma has a place in American culture.

Goffman mentions three types of stigmata: (1) physical deformity, (2) blemishes of individual character, and (3) tribal stigma of race, nationality and religion.[3] In the inner city we can find many people who carry more than one of these negative signs. Stigma are, however, not limited to people, as is usually thought. The concept of stigma can also be used to analyze places that are inhabited, or used, by different kinds of stigmatized people. The stigma of certain people can be transferred from their persons to the place that they occupy, or are thought to occupy, and alternatively, people can be stigmatized due to their choice of, or coerced residence in, a particular place. Common examples of this reflective relationship between place and self-identity are the leper colony, the ghetto and the prison.

In pre-modern society, lepers were not simply thought of as people with medical afflictions, but those who had been singled out by God, or gods, to be punished for their immoral transgressions. Similarly, historical and modern ethnic, racial and religious ghettoes are not seen by outsiders merely as places where people of like minds and needs congregate, but as areas of the city where strange and potentially "evil" people live. The social and psychological handicaps produced by living within the ghetto have most notably been studied by Louis Wirth and Kenneth B. Clark.[4] We might also consider that the stigma of an "ex-con" is related more to the fact of his having spent time within a prison, than having been convicted of committing a crime.[5]

Self-image and community image become integrated via the medium of our "home," and as noted by Clare Cooper, our place of residence is a symbol of our self.[6] Essentially, our place of residence attests to, or belies, our claims of any particular social status or amount of prestige. We can be either stigmatized or celebrated for our address.

People want to, and are supposed to, live in a community with others. In modern society, the "Search and Quest" for community has been extensively discussed by Digby Baltzell, Robert A. Nisbet, Roland Warren and many others.[7] Nisbet noted:

> In the same way that older theatrical problems of change and mobility had behind them, historically and logically moral aspirations to progress, so contemporary theoretical problems are given drive and meaning by moral aspirations toward community. (1953:29)

Along with Nisbet many other social scientists have intimated that establishing the existence of community, or community membership in the modern world, is a moral or normative problem. Roland Warren, a major community theorist, has gone so far as to say that community is a normative prescription for social action.[8] Each society has standards-- values and norms--for creating its own ideal residential community, and all members of that society are expected to live up to those standards. A critical discussion of the Anglo-American community model has been provided by N. Dennis, in which he attempted to explode some of the working myths of the historically utopian neighborhood community.[9] Despite his dissection of the myth of neighborhood life, and my own work on the myth of community,[10] ordinary people still feel the pressure to compare their local situations to what we might refer to as the "idealized normal" community settings. Social scientists

149

also continue to treat the theory of community as though it were an historical reality.

Unfortunately, the opportunity to approach the ideal of the American community is not available to many segments of our society. People who live in cities, particularly their inner recesses, minority group members and the poor are especially disadvantaged in the "quest for community." Also, the prevalence of the "anti-urban bias" in Anglo-American culture seems to make stigma an unavoidable feature of most urban neighborhood living.[11] An exception to this rule of thumb for city living might be made for those whom Robert K. Merton called "Cosmopolites," people who do not think of themselves as being socially restricted to their immediate environs, but who see themselves as "citizens of the world."[12] When the Prospect-Lefferts-Gardens area became highly urbanized in the 1930s, for example, wealthy Manorites were able to think of their homes as their "town houses" rather than their primary residence.

There are, of course, in all cities "classy" neighborhoods in which upper-class people with their economic and political advantages need not concern themselves with ordinary social stigma; in fact, they may find the "sinful" reputation of the city attractive. These "classy" Gold Coasts, Knob Hills, Beacon Hills and Park Avenues of American cities are essentially the exceptions that prove the rule of urban neighborhood stigmata. For when the rich vacate their posh surroundings, the areas become potential victims of rapid urban blight. Alternately, wherever the wealthy re-congregate, the neighborhood changes from stigmatized to celebrated.

Very important aspects of the social reality of community are physical appearances that are imbued with moral qualities by observers. Some of the simplistic, working assumptions about neighborhood community appearances can be stated as relationships such as: cleanliness-godliness, physical order-moral order, and good taste-good upbringing. It may be easy for scientists to scoff at these notions, but they cannot be ignored, for they are part of a common-sense nexus of everyday social explanations and interpretations. These simple formulas are social givens, accepted by people as valid, and are therefore "real" in their subjective experiences. It appears, for example, that activists in any community are inordinately concerned with cleanliness and beauty. In the worst slums of the city, when community organizations are formed they initiate block clean-ups, beautification contests and, invariably, they plant trees or other symbols of the "good community" life. The connection of the ideal version of the American community with middle-class, rustic virtues and accessories is shown in displays of respectability using visual and other sensory cues. Community is, therefore, an aesthetic as well as an ethical accomplishment. The values of community are assumed to be reflected in local physical appearances. A tour of anyone's community is best performed on a warm sunny day.

An example of this overwhelming concern by community activists with neighborhood propriety was demonstrated by the actions and thinking of Mrs. Baker, a local black community leader. She has a charitable conception of community activities, and devotes her time to helping others whom she feels are in need of her assistance. Not surprisingly, her husband is a minister, as was her father in the South, where she had lived prior to moving to New York. In the 1960s, she and her family moved to Bedford-Stuyvesant, a neighborhood in Brooklyn that is considered by many as one huge slum.13

When she first moved onto the block, it was "in bad shape." She felt that it was because her neighbors had lost "pride" in themselves and their neighborhood. The streets were dirty, with garbage "all over the place." She firmly believed that it was her "duty" to do her best regardless of the circumstances, and that others would be obliged to follow her good example. In conversations with her and her family it became clear that this moral dictum was, in a sense, their family "guiding light" and a commitment that led them through poverty and racial discrimination to a comfortable, middle-class life style. It should be noted that, in many black inner city neighborhoods, the Baker family is an "ideal type," in the Weberian sense of the term. It is people like the Bakers who form the core of many inner-city grass-roots community organizations that contradict the stereotype of blacks as apathetic to their deteriorating surroundings.

Immediately upon moving into her home, she set out to stimulate her neighbors to make their street the "cleanest, safest and most beautiful block possible." Of course, she tried to influence people by personal example.

> You see in the summer evening, when I started with the house and I started cleaning, they would say, "You work for the Sanitation Department?" And I said "Yes." (She wore a blue visiting nurse's uniform.) I had this broom and I said, "This condition is going to stop." "I want it clean." So I started on the porch, and went around the side of the house and swept it out. And I looked across the street and someone was hosing their house, and it hadn't been done before!
>
> So one day a little boy came up to me and asked, He said, "Miss, why you do things like that?" I said, "Do you see that (street-)light up there? That's me."

According to Mrs. Baker, her efforts also had an effect on the city sanitationmen who had been less than conscientious about servicing the street. After the residents kept the street cleaner, the sanitation-men began to "respect" her and her friends, according to Mrs. Baker. This is an interesting observation, in that a common complaint of inner city nonwhites is the neglect by city employees and agencies of their neighborhoods.

Having observed city sanitationmen in black neighborhoods in New York City, I can attest to the fact that they often leave the block in worse condi-tion than they found it--spilling garbage from cans and not sweeping up after themselves as they are officially required to do. During my research I have spoken with local garbagemen, and overheard their conversations in the coffee shops they frequent on their numerous "breaks." These men, black and white, are in a "status-income dilemma" as they perform their jobs. Ray Gold, in a study of janitor-tenant rela-tions in apartment houses, noted that one of the compensations for the lower status of the janitor is the higher status of the clients he serves.[14] The low-status worker is less humiliated by serving those he or she admires. The bias against nonwhites and inner city residents is well documented.[15] New York City sanitationmen, most of whom are white, all

of whom earn good salaries, and many of whom reside
in the suburbs are especially humiliated by having
to serve blacks.

Characteristically, the sanitationmen blamed
inner city deterioration completely on the personal
habits of blacks and other nonwhites who occupied the
areas. As in the case of Mrs. Baker's block, where
people extended themselves to keep it clean, they
remarked on those streets and the people who took
"good care" of the block. For example, they
referred to the "pigs" in some neighborhoods who do
not put their refuse in bags or cans, but merely
piled it up outside their buildings on the sidewalks,
and compared them to the people in "good" areas who
put out their garbage only on assigned days, neatly
wrapped and not overflowing onto the ground. The
example of Mrs. Baker, and the conversations of
sanitationmen, although by no means overwhelming,
is evidence that people often communicate to each
other via the medium of their environment, although
they may not communicate with each other verbally.

Urban neighborhoods can be defined in terms of
their physical attributes--buildings and streets.
We can speak of their objective histories and their
demographic characteristics. Another, and perhaps
more fruitful, analysis of urban neighborhoods could
be made by converting these attributes into symbolic
terms. We could try to provide accounts of neighborhoods without obliterating, through objectification,
the contexts and meanings assigned to those
attributes by the members of the community itself,
and those who come into direct contact with the area
through the course of time. For example, we know
that Bedford-Stuyvesant is now a predominately
"black" community, but we should be interested as
to why so many people assume, knowing little more
about the area than this "fact," that it is also a
bad neighborhood." What people "think" they know
about a community is often more dangerous to it than
those conditions which actually exist.

Even the "fact" that Bedford-Stuyvesant is a
black area has an interesting symbolic history. It
is not so important that an area, objectively outlined and named Bedford-Stuyvesant, contains a
majority of people who can be classified as black.
Originally in Brooklyn, there were two separate
communities, Bedford and Stuyvesant. In the 1950s,

when blacks started to move into these communities
in large numbers, the media responded by naming the
black community "Bedford-Stuyvesant." Blacks had
actually lived for many years in these two communities.
There were also several small "black towns" in this
part of Brooklyn during the early 1800s. When the
area was later urbanized, the local black population
was at first overwhelmed by white migrants to the
area's recently built brownstones and apartment
houses. Then, when the area began its decline, in
the 1950s, blacks began replacing whites who fled to
the suburbs and other parts of Brooklyn. Subsequently, as blacks spilled over the limited Bedford-
Stuyvesant boundaries into nearby neighborhoods,
Bedford-Stuyvesant grew to mean any place in Brooklyn
in which blacks dominated. This is similar to the
symbolic meaning of the name "Harlem" for all of
Manhattan's black population. The phenomenon of
changing mental maps of ethnic communities supports
the contention that neighborhoods are symbolic as
well as geographical areas.

A common image of the inner city is that of a
pathological environment. To most people the term
"inner city" conjures up scenes of crime, violence
and dirt, and deterioration. Although there are
certainly many parts of the nation's central cities
that deserve such a description, inner cities are by
no means homogeneous disaster areas. However, because
of this general perception of the central cities,
public and private agencies find greatest support
for drives to "redevelop" these segments of urban
society. Programs to "preserve" an inner city
community are almost unheard of. "Redevelopment"
means the demolition and then the reconstruction of
the inner city to fit predefined criteria of social
acceptability. In the main, this optimum environment
is based upon an historically, architecturally and
otherwise culturally biased model of community.

Not only are the physical arrangements of the
inner city neighborhood rejected, e.g., the grid
pattern of streets common to most American cities,
but also the types of social activities performed in
these settings are often defined as culturally
aberrant. Even the old-fashioned white-ethnic
neighborhood, somewhat idealized in American folklore,
is viewed as only a transitory phase in the process
of full Americanization. Their value as "curiosities"
is highlighted in cities with important tourist

industries. In these cities, there is some effort
to preserve the "Chinatowns" and "Little Italies,"
not because they are culturally desirable, but
because they are economic assets to the tourist trade.

Numerous social agencies are involved in the
planned modification of inner-city life styles. To
many of them the spontaneous and "disorganized" street
life of central city communities is viewed as a deviant version of American culture, a culture which
contains a distinct preference for a more organized,
stable community organization. The street life
observed in low-income black and Hispanic areas of
the city is culturally shocking to white middle-class
Americans. Herbert Gans and Jane Jacobs have extensively discussed these cultural biases of city
planners and others who try to impose their views
of "proper" local community life on inner-city
residents.[16]

The pressures for inner-city neighborhood
modification come not only from seemingly sinister,
monolithic agencies of social engineering; pressure
for change and the negative view of most city living
is generated from other, more subtle sources. For
example, through documentary and fictional accounts
presented in the mass media, we are presented daily
with a preferred vision of local social life. Also,
the media in commercials and advertisements, emphasize
the distinction between "normal" (ideal) and deviant
or stigmatized communities--basically suburbs and
inner city respectively.

There is an intervening twist to the view of
the happy, healthy people, living in detached homes
surrounded by trees and the crime and violence that
invariable is set in the central city during television
shows. During the 1960s, when black communities
across the country erupted as a response to racial
oppression and the death of Martin Luther King, viewers
were treated by scenes of Harlem, Newark and Detroit,
and saw "ghettoes" as they expected them to be--
citified. Yet the scenes of Watts in Los Angeles,
where one of the worst urban riots occurred, clearly
had a major dramaturgical flaw. The Watts community
is in many ways suburban in appearance, with block
upon block of detached homes, and lawn yards. Many
people could not understand that "those people" were
rioting about because "from the pictures" it looked
like a "good community." Poverty and oppression,

155

crime and violence are associated in the minds of
people with dense urban environments. Given this
common perception of the inner city, it is not
surprising that local people reject their own situations after they hold up their own neighborhood and
compare it to the template of the ideal, and find it
lacking.

Along with the projected pathological character
of the urban neighborhood, there are special stigma
that are connected to particular attributes of local
areas within urban systems. First among them in a
racially conscious society, such as our own, is the
decreased moral value and increased pathological
expectations for areas within cities that have large
nonwhite populations. A foreigner who studied the
literature on cities in the United States would,
through no fault of his own, assume that a necessary
characteristic of nonwhite communities are severe
social problems in the form of crime, drug addiction,
family disorganization and political apathy. If we
consider the native American looking for accounts of,
let us say, black neighborhoods in the more popular
literature, it is obvious why so many people carry
negative images of these urban neighborhoods.
According to the stereotype many urban communities
are burdened by nonwhite "sappers."

Achievement and Residential Movement

There are other aspects of American culture that
are related to the stigmatization of inner-city neighborhoods. American culture is extremely achievement-
oriented. Residential mobility and location are
often used as common-sense indicators of social
"success" and "failure." Some of the greatest
problems in maintaining the stability of the Lefferts
Manor, Prospect-Lefferts-Gardens and other city neighborhoods are the result of generational turnover. In
America, it is common for parents, relatives and
friends to convince the younger generation that their
success in life will, to a great degree, be demonstrated to others by their ability to move out of
their home neighborhood, and upward via geographic
mobility to a "better" community. For the upwardly
mobile middle-class and lower-middle-class whites
symbolic relocation has been accomplished in the past
by urban to suburban migration. More recently, the
growing black middle-class population has begun to

participate in this aspect of the "American Dream,"
by moving to the suburbs which have traditionally
been off-limits to them.

For most people, living close to childhood
friends is taken as an indication of family, ethnic
group, and individual failure. In "mainline" communities, of course, this generalization does not
hold. Elite areas are the type that people wish to
remain in, and others are trying to get into in order
to demonstrate that they have socially and economically "arrived." Also, among the un-Americanized the
drive to move out of the neighborhood of birth is not
as great as with most other Americans.[17] The ethnic
neighborhood, of first and second generation people,
continues to be an important aspect of their members'
social identity and style of life until they become
socialized into American community values. The
younger generation, more likely to be socialized
into American ways often become marginal members
of their ethnic community. The ideal of residential
mobility in American myth and folklore is a powerful
force which affects the distribution of population
across the maps of our cities and suburbs. There is
little doubt that this pervasive attitude--holding
residential mobility as an index of social worth--
is central to the problem of urban blight when viewed
from an intergenerational perspective.[18]

Urban residential communities become more prone
to destabilization when homes are no longer seen as
places in which to stay, maintain and defend. They
are then more likely to be treated as temporary
platforms from which to launch one's self and one's
children to better positions, and therefore better
places in society. It is not surprising that neighborhoods appear to decay at a faster rate once a
sizable age-cohort reaches middle-age: children are
sent off, those that can, move, and only those that
cannot leave remain behind to inhabit second-rate
settings.[19] Staying behind leads to negative images
of self, as transferred from the negatively defined
environment of "failure." To residual residents
their surroundings are no longer worthy of conscientious care. This change in attitude toward the
environment occurs because the "significant others"
of community members have passed through, and gone
to better residential places. The "shame" of one's
residence decreases the desire to invest psychological and economic capital in the neighborhood.

Residual neighborhood residents may begin to
see themselves as "inmates" in a place they would
rather not be. The "achievers" who have moved but
retain local property find it easier, because it is
no longer part of their personal identity to do to
their ex-home what they would not do before--to exploit
or "mine" their property keeps only its economic
value. We might say that this is another side of
urban "disenchantment" with the environment.
Achievers tend to be little concerned with the
resulting deterioration in the area, unless it
affects return on investments. They change their
definition of the site from a "home" to a "place of
business," and they try to extract as much from their
holdings as possible, and give as little as possible
to the territory in return.[20] To landlords, this is
the "proper" course of action, for they feel morally
bound to make a profit. In extreme cases, the
property is milked dry by non-payment of taxes and
other bills that cut into profits. The last resort,
available to those who still have insurance coverage,
is to "torch" the building and collect the last
drop of revenue from the neighborhood in the form
of insurance payments. The deserts of American
inner-city ghettoes, in essence, were once over-
grazed pastures.

Residual neighborhood residents take the
destruction of their neighborhoods as fatalistically
as Bengali monsoon flood victims; they believe that
it is some form of divine justice. They argue that,
if successful people deserve their rewards, then
failures deserve their punishments. To them this is
only logical given the achievement system into which
they have been socialized. Where once a single
family lived in relative comfort in Prospect-Lefferts-
Gardens, we now can often find two, three or perhaps
four families living in the same space. Overcrowded
buildings provide the owner of the property with the
revenue to maintain his respectable residence in
suburban or ex-urban society.

The depersonalization and rationalization of
the community by the absentee landlord often proceeds
to the creation of real estate management corporations
to collect rents and deal with tenants. One tries
not to "pollute" oneself by dealing directly with the
"harajani" (Hindu untouchable caste) of American
society. Inheritors of rental property in Prospect-
Lefferts-Gardens may not be aware of the exact

location of their source of revenue. To them it is usually "over there" in the ghetto, where it "used to be a nice neighborhood." "What those people did to that area" is an often heard comment about neighborhoods in which people once lived.

Some owners of property may not have a generational tie to the community, and so they find it easier to see their property in purely economic terms. To these, a whorehouse, pornographic bookstore or drug clinic--which carry great social stigma--are rational possibilities. "Who lives in the inner city?" they may ask. The answers they hear are invariable: no one, nobodies, renters, welfare clients who move from place to place going nowhere, and old people on pensions and social security, or new immigrants who are looking for "anyplace" to live. The poor move from one residential dropping to another--places that were once homes and neighborhoods, that became launching pads, holdings and eventually slums.

The gestation of a slum, which generally takes several generations, is essentially the result of defections from community ideals. As a place becomes less of a community it correspondingly becomes more of a slum. The neighborhood community is produced in many ways. Most often we think of it as a set of local institutions and a resident population with certain socio-economic characteristics. Symbolically, as a "performance," it can be acted out by following appropriate rules of conduct on a "proper" stage. Community can also be created in retrospect by describing and explaining past events. Community activists and organizers try to create contemporary community realities. The elderly tell stories of the "good old days" in the same area. All methods for creating community demand that people assign meanings and intentions to observable or phantasized phenomena, and that community proponents search for symbols of community which will be appreciated by their audiences. For example, meanings and intentions can be assigned to streets and buildings which can affect the "possibility" of community in any particular location; a whorehouse or a fire-gutted building are not community-like objects, while tree-lined streets and well-kept homes are.

Mrs. Baker created community by performing acts that conformed to the community expectations of both her neighbors and their garbagemen. People and things

159

in an area might be thought of as "appearances" that form an experiential matrix for assessing the reality of community.[21] Talk, physical objects, gestures, skin colors, etc., are signs in the urban environment that are transformed into symbols as they are experienced, interpreted, and given meanings and intentions by observers.[22]

The existence of community as a social reality is problematic in the inner city, even when it is taken-for-granted by local residents. This is because the production of community is the result of a continuous and retrospective process--a sort of constant comparative analysis undertaken by ordinary people in their environments. The process is best seen when community, as a possibility, is threatened. It then becomes necessary for those who wish to maintain it to "prove it," by accentuating local appearances which are thought to lead to confirmation by audiences. The opposite is also true: those who wish to destroy a community will highlight those facts which are inconsistent with the cultural ideal of the "normal" community.

Very simply, in America the small town, rural or suburban neighborhood is the idealized normal. The inner-city neighborhood is the stigmatized deviant, and if the area features minority group members and other culturally defined negative attributes, such as large apartment houses, it is super-stigmatized. This definition of the inner-city neighborhood, which is an objective description laced with culturally prescribed valuations, then becomes part of the social identity of the neighborhood and of its residents.

The Moral Careers of Inner-City Residents

What are the possible social and psychological responses of people who live in the inner city to the stigma of their residential location? Goffman notes that:

> . . . people who have a particular stigma
> tend to have similar learning experiences
> regarding their plight, and similar
> changes in conception of self--a similar
> "moral career" that is both cause and

effect of commitment to a similar sequence
of personal adjustments. (1963:32)

Goffman also argues that there can be several
different moral careers that evolve out of various
patterns of adjustment and socialization in regard
to the same stigma. Different responses to the same
stigma may also come about because people may not
have in common other important social characteristics. For example, in Prospect-Lefferts-Gardens
all share the stigma of living in an inner-city
nonwhite neighborhood, but black residents and
white residents, young and old, rich and poor,
react somewhat differently to their collective
social blemish.

Through observing the residents of the
Lefferts Manor and Prospect-Lefferts-Gardens over
several years, at least four general categories of
adjustment to the stigma, placed on the neighborhood
by insiders and outsiders alike, became crystallized:
(1) Unawares, (2) Failures, (3) Achievers, and
(4) Activists. These "Four Moral Careers of Inner
City Residents," I believe, are generalizable to the
residents of other neighborhoods which are experiencing
now, or have experienced in the past, ethnic change
and physical deterioration. Fortunately for the
residents of Prospect-Lefferts-Gardens neighborhood
and the Lefferts Manor, they have many positive
aspects and a large number of Activists and therefore have not entered into the advanced stages of
urban blight.

1) The Unaware

There are many recent immigrants to the United
States, and Prospect-Lefferts-Gardens, who are unaware
of their own, and their new neighborhood's stigma.
Other immigrants are aware of the stigma, but do not
"appreciate" it due to lack of socialization into
American community values. To those poorest
immigrants from the shantytowns of the Caribbean or
South America, and more recently from the slums of
Hong Kong, the rooms they occupy in decaying buildings
on the fringe of the neighborhood are, relatively
speaking, symbols of upward mobility. The most
pitiful of the Unawares are the illegal aliens who
not only are grateful for anyplace to stay, but are
immobilized by fear of detection when they realize

how dangerous their living conditions are; landlords often threaten to bring them to the attention of the Immigration and Naturalization Service.

Another group of Unawares are the welfare clients--families and individuals who, in many cases, have lived in slums for most of their lives and have so internalized their personal stigma that it is an unconscious part of their personality. Identity problems arise for them only on those rare occasions when they confront "normals," such as social workers. These people tend to accept their situations and do little to change and improve local conditions. Their low status also limits the number of times they meet outsiders and outside institutions which might motivate them toward self-improvement. Welfare clients are frequently so personally demoralized that they are easily exploited by local landlords.

To a degree, the smiles on the faces of ghetto residents while firemen vainly try to extinguish blazes at "torched" buildings are an indication of vicarious revenge for their ill-treatment. Fire department officials report that many suspicious fires in low-income areas are set by welfare clients seeking relocation and new furniture allotments, in addition to fires set for "revenge." These actions indicate an understandable disaffection for the local environment on the part of the very poor in society. The low-income ghetto resident, and the poor immigrant, are two types of people who dissolve into the masses of the polluted inner-city neighborhood.

Some authors have "romanticized" the neighborhood life of the modern urban poor, as earlier writers have written of the contented European serfs, ghetto Jews, and in our own history, the happy slaves of southern plantations.23 We often hear of the vibrance and richness of ghetto street life. It should be noted that poor people, as human beings, always try to make their environments as bearable as possible, and that the richness of local social life in ghettoes is not an indication of contentment. Also, the low-income ghetto is furthered stigmatized by the local cultural life that develops because it is viewed by outsiders as "abnormal."

It is difficult for outsiders to appreciate the culturally prescribed activities of low-income people

toward their inner-city environments. Unromantically,
to the ghetto residents the activities of youths
throwing rocks through school windows or the looting
of a burned-out liquor store are "appropriate"
behaviors supported by local community values and
norms. Although we do not find these activities in
Prospect-Lefferts-Gardens to any great degree, in
neighborhoods not too far away such is not the case.

(2) The Failure

The Failure is a person who accepts the stigma
of the neighborhood in which he or she lives,
"appreciates" its cultural content, and aspires to
the community ideal, but who is unable to move away
to better surroundings. In many ways the Failures
are like the "losers" studied by Elliot Liebow in his
Tally's Corner (1967) community study. Failures are
also frequently psychologically and socially unable
to blend into changed or changing communities. The
elderly poor are a major component of the residential
failures in American cities today. Others are the
unemployed, and people who are generally handicapped
in their pursuit of the "American Dream."[24]

Failures can be divided into two relatively
dangerous types for the community. One type of
Failure aims to destroy only his or her self. The
other tries to destroy the neighborhood in which he
or she lives. All Failures attempt to dissociate
themselves from the "new" community when they feel
the area has changed. They try to show through
their actions that they are not part of this new
community, that they do not "belong" there.
In the conversations of these people on the
streets and in local stores, they can be heard
"talking down" the area and playing up its stigma.
They also provide themselves with excuses for being
"trapped" such as: "I can't afford to move now"
and "I'm only staying here because my rent is so
low." The reason for their attempts to symbolically
destroy the area is that to them "their" community
has already been desecrated. Some engage in self
and community flagellation as a way to atone for
their sins and to purify the territory.[25]

The Failures in Prospect-Lefferts-Gardens
cause community organizations and activists a great
deal of trouble. Not only are they unwilling to

join in efforts to solve community problems, they are also the constant bearers of bad news about the area, and they seem to "enjoy" spreading hopelessness and despair--emotions that they see as appropriate for the local situation. They also mock the efforts of their neighbors to maintain local appearances. To the Failure, all efforts toward saving the community, or bringing it back to life are not futile but also "sacreligious."

An example of this destructive attitude vis-a-vis the Lefferts Manor is appropriate here. In New York and other cities, there has been a rapid growth of block associations, which are small-scale community organizations, in the inner city. They engage in many activities to promote community spirit and improve physical surroundings. On one street in the Manor, the block association scheduled a collective effort to sweep the street and clean out basements of accumulated debris. In order to do this, they closed off the street to traffic and had a party afterwards to reward participants. Several Failures on the block complained to police and other authorities that the activity was a "public nuisance" and demanded that it be stopped. They also refused to park their cars on another street during the "sweep-up" so that residents could clean near the curbs.

Some neighborhood Failures are in especially advantageous positions to negatively affect community morale. One woman, who with her husband owned a coffee shop near the Lefferts Manor, constantly complained to her customers about how the neighborhood was "going to the dogs." As time went by, more of her regular customers either died or moved away. As the community became blacker in composition her diatribes about the decline of the area became "coded." She spoke of "welfare" people who were ruining the apartment houses. Her regular customers knew that she was talking about blacks in general; so did local blacks, who avoided her place.

As her patrons diminished, her business subsided until, when she decided to sell the store, it was not doing well enough to attract interested buyers. Several times she had been asked by patrons why, if she did not like the neighborhood, she had not sold it and moved away. She explained that she was sending her son to a medical school in Florida, and that she

164

needed the money. When her son failed out of school,
she quickly sold the store for a low price and
moved. During the months shortly before she left,
she was especially bitter and ascerbic about the
area, as she punished the community for her own
failures. She had earlier complained that her son
had difficulty getting into medical school because
of "preferences" given to blacks.

One of the natural phenomena that helps a
community to change is aging. The oldtimers in the
Lefferts Manor remember the community in its heyday.
As residues of traditional community elites, they
comprise a special group of residential failures.
Even small changes in the Manor are, to them,
symbolically significant. The future prospects for
the community are in large part dependent on their
attitudes, as it is their homes that are likely to
be sold in the near future. People can die either
gracefully or ungracefully. Ungracefully, one can
view the approach of death as indication of a battle
lost--what Ernest Becker in his Denial of Death (1973)
called the failure of the "sui generis project."
Friends die off at an increasing rate; no one comes
to visit; family members scatter. The world changes,
and its new shape is unfriendly and frightening.
Older people then retreat into themselves and their
homes, which can remind them of what they once were.

Some become bitter and self-destructive. They
try to destroy themselves and reminders of the past,
or they abandon them. They neglect their persons
and those things that once were sources of pride.
When death is right around the corner, there is no
more need to maintain appearances. When you go, the
house, the block, the community goes with you. The
homes of the defeated elderly mirror their self-
image--old, dilapidated and desperate. Fortunately
for the community, few of the aged go through this
dehumanizing process at the same time.

Of course, it is possible to react differently
to the facts of life and death--to maintain one's
self and home. It is, however, difficult to maintain
self-respect for the aged in a youth-oriented culture
where people spend thousands of dollars to remove
signs of age that once were symbols of dignity and
respect. Some oldtimers is the neighborhood go
overboard in trying to maintain themselves and
their property. On one street an elderly white

man and black woman sweep the curbs of their block
from end to end every morning. Others are exceptionally well groomed and dressed, and keep immaculate
homes. These aging "pillars of the community" have
not given up in the face of racial change and other
symbols of decline. But, behind their exemplary
facades they also believe that the neighborhood is
"not what it used to be."

The elderly Manorites are most offended by
community change because of their great psychic
investments there. When injured by newcomers, they
retaliate by symbolic acts of destruction. Their
talk of the Manor is filled with uncomplimentary
phrases and comparisons which accentuate the negative
aspects of the present and highliaht the positive
virtues of the past--before "they" started moving in.
They refuse to participate in constructive Association
activities, but show up for every meeting which
focuses on crime and decay in the area. There, they
publically vent their anger and then insist that
"nothing can be done" to save the community. They
isolate themselves from newcomers and form coteries
of critics which seem to take pleasure in each new
flaw and fault in the fabric of the neighborhood.
These people also gradually retreat from the Manor
social scene, a preparation for eventually selling
their homes to real estate brokers who "they know"
will not respect the Manor covenant. They want the
highest price for their property, regardless of the
consequences for the community, because to them it
is already "a lost cause." These are the same
people who, years earlier, might have complained of
one-family zone violations--people who fought to enter
the Lefferts Manor against religious and ethnic discrimination, struggled to maintain the elite character
of the area during their productive years. Now,
vindictively they try to insure that future Manorites
will lose a valuable legacy.

(3) The Achievers

Many of the Achievers in Prospect-Lefferts-
Gardens are what Herbert Gans termed "middle-class
mobiles"--those who model themselves on middle-class
outsiders, and therefore "detach themselves from
relatives and old friends and are often rejected
by these."[26] The Achiever accepts the stigma of the
neighborhood, aspires to the community ideal and has

the means to escape to a normal community. The major difference between Failures and Achievers is this ability to leave. The Achievers form the ranks of the mass or staggered flight from changing communities. Generally, it is the more affluent, and the more prominent residents of a neighborhood who are the first to leave. The Achiever is a danger to the community because of their decreased concern with whom replaces them, and the general fate of the area. They are also not psychologically tied (trapped) to the community as the Failure; therefore their actions are likely to be less spiteful. The Achiever sees the neighborhood as a "lost cause," but also they seem to have a slight sense of guilt for abandoning it. Often the guilt is demonstrated by secretiveness concerning their impending move, and their reluctance to let neighbors know of their intention to sell their home, or move out of their apartments. As an example, one young professional couple, who had been very active in local community associations for several years, "all of a sudden" stopped attending community meetings and turned down invitations to parties with neighbors. A few months after the cessation of community activity, moving vans were seen in front of their house, and then they were gone. If you can engage then in conversations about the neighborhood, Achievers have very little good to say about the area, and a great deal positive to say about communities elsewhere--most often in the suburbs. As the time for moving out approaches, statements about the relative merits of neighborhood become exaggerated.[27] Achievers are busy rationalizing their decision to change their residence.

As noted, the problems that Achievers create for a neighborhood come from their diminished concern for the area. One man in Prospect-Lefferts-Gardens was selling his house on a street just outside of the Lefferts Manor that consisted of small one-family homes occupied by working-class families. His neighbors "knew" that he was planning to sell because they saw "people coming to visit on Saturday mornings." Most people in the area do not have visitors on Saturday mornings unless they are doctors or dentists, with home offices. The owner, however, refused to allow his neighbors, who had prospective buyers for the houses, to contact his real estate broker. The owner was white and most of his neighbors were middle-class blacks, who were afraid that the

building would be converted into a rooming house
and thereby "ruin" the block.

Selling the house to a speculator, or rooming
house operator, might not only bring a higher price
for the property, the seller thinks, but such buyers
have an easier time gaining money for the purchase
price than ordinary people. The reason for this
situation is that black or changing communities
are invariably red-lined by banks. "Red-lining"
means that certain areas are seen by banks and
other lending institutions as bad risk areas. (The
results of a 1976 New York Public Interest Group
Study of red-lining is shown in Map 13.) They therefore refuse to grant mortgage loans to prospective
buyers, make the terms of the loan impossible for
middle-class people, or limit the life of the loan
or the amount of principal. Speculators and other
businessmen generally have other sources of funds
and do not rely on the normal ways for purchasing
property in the inner city. The result of red-lining
is that families who would be assets to a neighborhood
are prevented from moving in. Inner-city block-
busting and red-lining are generally concomitant
phenomena.

The owner of the house in question, convinced
that the area was already on the decline, thought
only of his own financial needs and sold his house
to an agent who promptly converted it to a rooming
house. Actions, such as these, accelerate physical
deterioration and help along the self-fulfilling
prophecy of the inevitable decay of changing
neighborhoods. Racism and racial fears make
it possible to correlate decline with white to
nonwhite racial change. Few people, including
many blacks themselves, discriminate between
classes and types of nonwhite residents. Urban
blight is often "explained" by estimates of minority
group influx into a community. These explanations
support the argument that nonwhite people in
America are not viewed as members of ethnic or class
groups, but of "castes." In white single-family home
areas of cities across the country, people assume that
any black homebuyer automatically will convert the
home for multiple-family use in order to afford to
keep it.

The awareness of this bias and the repugnance
of the nonwhite community stigma make it easy to

Map 13. REDLINING BY MAJOR SAVINGS BANKS
IN BROOKLYN, 1976.

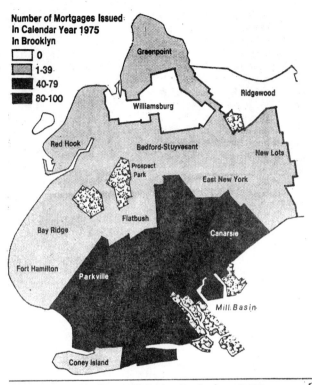

**Number of Mortgages Issued
In Calendar Year 1975
In Brooklyn**

- ☐ 0
- ▨ 1-39
- ▩ 40-79
- ▦ 80-100

Mortgages issued by the seven largest savings banks on owner-occupied residential properties in Brooklyn in 1975

BANK	NUMBER OF MORTGAGES ISSUED	TOTAL DOLLAR Value of MORTGAGES ISSUED (In millions)	TOTAL ASSETS (In millions)	MORTGAGES AS PERCENT OF TOTAL ASSETS
Greenpoint Savings Bank	722	24.9	868	2.87
Metropolitan Savings Bank	69	3.0	1,034	0.28
East New York Savings Bank	48	1.9	864	0.21
Brooklyn Savings Bank	52	1.9	1,119	0.17
Dime Savings Bank of New York	184	5.3	3,777	0.14
Williamsburgh Savings Bank	67	1.9	1,877	0.01
Greater New York Savings	44	1.1	1,402	0.01
TOTAL	1,186	40.0	10,941	0.37

Source: New York Public Interest Research Group

From The New York Times, December 6, 1976: 37.

facilitate panic selling of homes. The block-busting real estate agent is a good social-psychologist; that agent knows what makes people worry and what induces them to move. Panic selling by whites in some sections of Prospect-Lefferts-Gardens in the 1960s, not only resulted in the loss of irreplacable good housing for the seller, but also the distrust of nonwhites in the community toward whites who remained. Blacks tend to see local whites as people who are "ready to move." Psychologically, some of the black professionals in the area felt extremely "insulted" when, after living in the community for a few years, it became predominately black. When they moved in, they heard that their neighbors were "afraid of them." The personal slight of the black middle class is further enhanced by the fact that many of those who moved away were working-class white ethnics, Italians and Irishmen, who lived a few blocks away from the Lefferts Manor.

The idea that working class whites fled from the presence of successful black lawyers and doctors is personally upsetting, given the belief of many socially mobile blacks that occupational prestige helps to overcome racial stigma. Upper-middle-class black Manorites seem to compensate for their racial stigma by being extraordinarily "class conscious." Few allow their children to play with working-class black children in the area, or to attend local schools which are filled with nonwhite and Hispanic pupils.

The problems created by Achievers for the Prospect-Lefferts-Gardens neighborhood does not end when they move away. Some Achievers come back periodically to visit friends and relatives who remain in the area. On these occasions they are quick to point out how much worse the area has become since they were last there. They invariably ask those they visit why they are still in the neighborhood, and how nice their own new neighborhood is compared to "here." Frequent statements which are made: "In my neighborhood, I'm not afraid to send my kids to public school"; "My wife can walk on the streets after dark"; "We can leave our door unlocked"; and "I don't have to worry about finding a parking space." Most of the Achievers who return to visit ignore the good things about the old neighborhood which still

170

exist, and focus on those things they know are "wrong." They seem to obtain a great deal of pleasure from invidious comparisons and making their hosts feel uncomfortable in their presence. Their "captive" hosts find it easier to agree with them about the relative merits of their respective communities, and offer the usual mea culpas for their sins such as: "I wish I could afford a house like yours." Achievers find it difficult to find fault with the Lefferts Manor; therefore they focus on less fortunate parts of the community for their comments.

(4) The Activists

Not everyone in Prospect-Lefferts-Gardens simply passively accepts its stigma, and adds to its problems. The Activist responds to the stigma by trying to upgrade the community. Although it may at first seem inconsistent, Activists accept the stigma of the area, appreciate it, agree with the ideal version of the American community, and, except for blacks, and members of racially integrated families, have the ability to move to just about any community they wish. They differ from other community members in their efforts to prove that the stigma is inaccurate, unjustified, or they try to change and improve the community in ways that bring it up to the standard of the "normal." They use emotional appeals to insiders and outsiders to help prevent destruction of their stigmatized community and engage in preventative and rehabilitative projects. Individual efforts are inspiring, but it is the organized efforts of community groups that hold out the greatest prospects for the survival of inner-city neighborhoods. In the past, there have been many examples of people who held out on their own in changing neighborhoods; they can best be described as "the last persons to leave."

The Community Paradigm

The methods for removing the stigma of the inner city are derived from the model of the ideal American community: clean, green and middle class. A schematic of the Community Paradigm is presented in Figure 2. The Activists, if we were to use Robert K. Merton's often-cited structural paradigm of goals and means,

171

are not "Rebels" but "Conformists."[28] In fact, all
of the community residents, except the "Unawares,"
accept the standard American community values, or
goals, and the legitimate means for attaining them.
Rebels, who reject both community goals and means
to attain them, are likely to become hermits. And
innovators, who accept the goals but reject the
means, tend to set up communes or other alternative
community structures.[29] Activists, very simply,
claim to have the ability to be "normal" in a deviant
setting. In the stigmatized community, though, this
act or performance, requires a great deal of skill
and effort because the stage is set with ideological
booby traps and social discrepancies.[30] It is
difficult for most people who appraise the "com-
munityness" of the inner city to equate, for
example, a rent strike meeting of Puerto Rican
welfare mothers, held in a tenement lobby, with our
sacred New England Town Hall traditions. It is also
difficult for most observers to realize that a poor
urban black family has roots in American culture at
least as deep as those of the Daughters of the
American Revolution. The cherished local American
community culture in the inner city is as out of
character, as are scenes of Black Santa Clauses
singing jingle bells on streetcorners, with a
calypso beat. Our American community traditions
are Mom, apple pie and baseball, not day care, bean
pies and schoolyard basketball games.

     Because of the importance of the Activists to
the Lefferts Manor, Prospect-Lefferts-Gardens and
neighborhoods like them in other cities, it is
necessary to discuss them and their activities in
greater depth and at greater length. The material
used in this section was gathered via intensive
interviews of fifteen community leaders in the
greater Prospect-Lefferts-Gardens neighborhood
during the early 1970s. Each interview lasted a
total of between six and twelve hours, two or more
three hour sessions. This time was needed in order
to plumb the depths of their feelings about their
community, and their motivations for involvement.
The effort was well-rewarded. In some cases the
interview sessions took on an almost "psychiatric"
tone, as subjects freely related their experience
in this and other neighborhoods in which they had
lived. It is generally understood that "true"
community leaders are extremely moralistic, and
have deep personal attachment to their homes and

their neighborhoods. The interviews confirmed this perception.

In every case of community activism in the inner-city neighborhood some real or imagined decline of the status of the neighborhood seems to have triggered the intense involvement. These same changes also set off the movement of Achievers out of the community. Two female black community leaders, who at one time were "pioneers" in the area, relate below both their reasons for wanting to move into Prospect-Lefferts-Gardens, and subsequently their reasons for community involvement:

> Activist 1:
>
> Well, my husband wanted to buy and we went to the real estate people. I didn't care about the schools because my children were in high school and didn't have to go in the area. I was interested in seeing what kinds of people were outside. . . . The apartment house across the street is [was] Puerto Ricans, Italians, Irish, all kinds. . . . I didn't like the house, but my husband said this was something "I really like." So I said "Alright. You don't like it, we can move again, that's all."
>
> Well, first of all it was mixed . . . and at the time it was nice, but what happened was people began to move out. The first time I was there it looked like a community, because it was a mixture, and you could see the beautification, the scenery. The people seemed to be getting along fine. They were friendly. They were sitting outside and when you passed they said "Hello." You could see the families . . . at the beginning it was clean. So after we moved in things changed. People began to get careless.

There are several comments that must be made on the reflections of Activist 1. First of all, she, like any other prospective home-buyer, shops around for a suitable neighborhood to live in, and considers all of its obvious good and bad points. For blacks, the selection is severely limited, so it is a choice between a small number of alternatives. Schools in the inner city are generally in horrendous conditions, but the local elementary schools were not important

173

Figure 2

Schema of Community Paradigm*

		Goals, or Values of the Ideal American Community: Accept-Available	Goals, or Values of the Ideal American Community: Reject-Unavailable
Norms, or Means to Attain the Goals of the Ideal American Community	Accept / Available	Conformist Achievers Failures Activists	Ritualist Failures Unawares Poor Minority Group members
	Reject / Unavailable	Innovator Communalists "Alternative Communities" Extraordinary Groups	Rebel-Retreatist Anarchists Hermits

*Based on Robert K. Merton's paradigm of Social Structure and Anomie (1968:185-248).

Notes: The "Ideal American Community" is middle-class, White-Anglo-Saxon, and rural or suburban in form. Failures accept both the goals and means of the community ideal, but may psychological dissociate themselves from the stigmatized neighborhood in order to save their "selves."

Poor minority group members, although they may accept the means to attain ideal community goals, may not have the means available to them.

to her because her children were high school age,
increasing the number of areas from which to choose.
Also, the "appearance" of the area is a significant
factor in evaluation of the neighborhood. Her
comments on what the area looked like brings to the
surface the substructure of American community values.
She said, "It looked like a community." It had
beauty, greenery and that people seemed friendly,
and their pride in the community was expressed
through a concern for cleanliness. Although it
has been difficult for social scientists to define
community, ordinary people simply see and feel it.[31]

Finally, we should note her interest in the
ethnic and racial "mixture" of people in the area,
which she saw as one of its positive aspects. We
would say that the area was "integrated," but as
the experienced sociologist and most ordinary people
know, integrated communities eventually become nonwhite communities. As she noted, "After we moved in
things changed." In all of my interviews and conversations with people in city neighborhoods, most
blacks and other minority group members saw an
"integrated" neighborhood in a positive light,
while very few whites felt the same way.

Activist 2:

I moved into the area because I was
informed the area was a strictly static,
interracial area. After we were here a
while I began to notice more whites moving
out, and I became concerned because I was
originally from "Bed-Stuy" [Bedford-
Stuyvesant], which was a beautiful area,
still is, but the minute a black family
moved in, a white moved out, or ten moved
out. . . . And I didn't want to see this
happen to this area because we have so
much invested in the area to see this
happen.
I felt that the only thing we could do
was to try to publicize the area and let
people know that this area existed, and
to try to get young whites to move in who
would be interested in preserving the
neighborhood and saving it from becoming
a ghetto.
Well, I had been going on "house tours"
[in brownstone neighborhoods] for about six

175

years prior to moving here, and I noticed the
caliber of people who went on house tours.
They were young, black and white--the people
who are interested in an area, and who felt
that this New York, Brooklyn, was a beautiful
place to live in and why see it go down the
drain? So that was my main idea--to get
people to preserve an area and build it up.
     For one thing, this is a beautiful area,
and it convinced people [the house tour did]
that it wasn't a decrepit area. . . . We are
an interracial community. We are, and still
are, stable, middle-class, and of course we
have our poor people too. . . . But, the people
who did buy into the area, the blacks that
buy houses, they have improved on them; which
I have been told by whites who have remained
--that they have improved on the houses,
inwardly and outwardly.

     It is apparent that Activist 2's deja vu of
community change stimulated her to get involved in
neighborhood projects. Living in the Lefferts Manor,
she found little support for the "house tours" she
was certain would show to outsiders the positive
qualities of the neighborhood. When she started, in
the late 1960s, Manorites, as always, were very
conservative and unwilling to publically admit their
problems. A few defeatists in the community were
influential enough in the Manor Association, she said,
to prevent her from gaining the support of the
organization. Therefore, she extended herself, and
the boundaries of her community, by going outside the
Manor for collaborators. These activists formed the
Prospect-Lefferts-Gardens Neighborhood Association
and joined with the Brooklyn Brownstone Conference
and the New York Brownstone Revival Committee in
their back-to-the-city movement activities.
Illustration 4 is a design for a house tour poster
and is a symbolic expression of neighborhood pride.

     Besides the more obvious points made in her
interview, there are several which might escape the
casual reader's eye. One item is the qualifications
that she places on residence of blacks in the neighborhood. Note that statements about blacks proceed
almost immediately from the statement about the poor
in the community. When speaking of black residents
it appears to be necessary to emphasize their
positive qualities, as though it would not be taken

Illustration 4. HOUSE TOUR POSTER OF MANOR HOUSE
BY HENRY O. BRODER

From Prospect-Lefferts-Gardens Association
Brochure, 1978.

for granted. Interviewing white residents in other
Brooklyn communities undergoing racial change, one
frequently runs across these kinds of statements and
qualifiers. In middle-class integrated areas, the
linguistic form seems to be, "Yes, we have blacks in
the area but they are nice people." It appears that
the question--"Do blacks live in your neighborhood?"--
implies that "black" means poor or problem people.
Also of great interest is the implication by similar
statements made by nonwhites about themselves that the
reference group for making evaluations is white middle
class society. It is very important that white people
approve of both the area and the people who live
there.

It is this perception of black and other nonwhite accommodations to white American community
values that raises the charge of "Uncle Tomism"
against some nonwhite community activists. Also, as
can be expected, a larger than normal proportion of
people involved in the back-to-the-city activities in
the Prospect-Lefferts-Gardens area are white, which
brings complaint that these activities are "racist."
It is fascinating to this writer that organizations
which aim to bring white people into a black neighborhood, or retaining those already there can so
easily be labelled "racist," while bringing black
families into white communities is seen in liberal
circles as "saintly." One thing seems certain:
racism and racial issues are the most common component of inner city life in Brooklyn.

It is important to emphasize that both
Activists noted above are different community
"types." The first Activist was a non-elite person,
less cosmopolitan in orientation--a "routine seeker--
to use Gans's typology of the Urban Villagers.[32]
People like her do not look beyond their immediate
environment and resources for solving community
problems. The second activist, a resident of the
elite Lefferts Manor, found it easier to go outside
the community and to join in city-wide and nationwide organizational efforts to preserve city
neighborhoods. For example, she and her colleagues
quickly joined the National Neighbors organization,
which is an association of integrated communities with
members in Detroit, Philadelphia and many other
American cities.

Ordinary people have difficulty in realizing that their personal community problems are shared by others and that problems have a better chance in being solved with collective, organized action. Part of the reluctance to join in large-scale community action stems from the feeling that people have that big organizations "swallow them up." This is part of the general fear of bureaucracy. Large-scale organizations are more likely to be seen by neighborhood residents as causes and not solutions of problems. Community issues are also personal, and organizations tend to overwhelm individuals, as noted in this interview with a community activist (white male) in the Lefferts Manor who dropped out of the back-to-the-city movement after attending several organization meetings:

> It was stuffy. The people I thought would go there would be more down to earth . . . but it had a kind of elite sort of atmosphere. They talked about the problems they had with houses and how much money they spent. The people seemed to be quite affluent. At first they may have been a different sort of people, but now I don't see them having any relationship to the grass roots movement now. I don't know why I feel that way. Just the <u>flavor</u> of it.

Community, then, is not only something that ordinary people "see" and "feel"; it is also something that has a distinct "flavor." To most people "community" means smallness, and few people are able to overcome their biases against big organizations and formal procedures. Most community residents prefer small groups and small-scale actions, such as getting the large pothole on the corner fixed, not having all the streets in the city repaved.

We should turn now to a consideration of the white families who moved in Prospect-Lefferts-Gardens as a result of the house tours. The people quoted also became active in various neighborhood associations. As we would expect, white families who would move into an integrated community, exhibit the moral career pattern of Activists, as they must personally deal with the social and psychological problems created by their choice of a stigmatized community. This is demonstrated constantly by their concern with how their friends, relatives and other outsiders evaluate their home environment. To

179

outsiders, white Activists in black neighborhoods are the strangest of all creatures.

Activist 3 (white female):

Everything was good [after they moved in]. Although the reactions one gets from Queens [a suburban fringe borough of New York] residents when one says that one is moving to Brooklyn are so horrendous, and so depressing. And ninety percent of them are euphemisns for one thing [blacks]. From the postman to the man in the delicatessen: "Brooklyn? What kind of neighborhood?" "How is it over there?" And just constant, everywhere we went we got that. The guy who took down the lighting fixture: "Is it all right over there?"

[Reactions of friends:] They have all been very impressed and we think we scored a few points. They're impressed with the block. Of course, we made a big issue of showing them the block. And they are impressed obviously with: number one the house, number two the price, number three the block, and number four the fact that our child is in public school, and that the whole neighborhood seems to be working and maybe it isn't quite a blackboard jungle or whatever.

Activist 4 (white male):

[Reactions of friends:] So far only four or five people have given me praise. One of them is a typical suburban couple who now live in the city, but can't wait to move into the suburbs because New York is "so bad," and the suburbs are "so good." So they would never move into the city. Another is the type that would want to live in the Canarsie or Mill Basin areas [two all-white Brooklyn neighborhoods]. . . . You know, with flashy furniture and wall-to-wall carpeting and that sort of thing [a conformist] . . . and they would not want to live here because it is not a fancy area or a well known area.

A lot of them are afraid. Right away they think that because there are a lot of blacks living here that it has to be full of drug addicts, and dangerous to live here, and automatically they figure that the homes are broken into.

It is clear from these and other interviews of white activists, most of whom live in the Manor, that they are concerned with the perceptions of outsiders, and that the racial composition of the neighborhood is the primary factor used in evaluations. Although most activists in stigmatized areas take rather defensive postures toward their denegration, essentially counter-punching negative comments about the area with positive ones that are not so "obvious" to outsiders, some Activists respond aggressively to assault by attacking the foundation of the ideal of suburban living. As shown in this interview with a Manor Activist (white male), who once lived in a Long Island suburb:

> I think this area is probably the finest. In House and Gardens magazine, a psychiatrist was quoted as saying that a row of houses exactly the same is the most beneficial because it provides an opportunity for closeness plus the fact that it offers separateness of having your own home. I find this to be true, because when I lived in Long Island in a ranch style house with all big open spaces and the neighbors everywhere were very cold. Everybody had their own barbecue, and their own driveway, and there was not any sharing whatsoever.
> In the suburbs people get the feeling that they are living on a separate island. Everybody has their own property. There was no sense of belonging to a group on the block. There was no sense of community spirit. There was nothing uniting anybody except their own lots. Everybody was into cutting their own grass, and into their own house. Very independent. There were no friends--no neighbors to count on.
> My concern is a continued development of action among people. There should be community spirit. If this can be done through a square dance or a block party, I think this would be good for community growth. People will feel less afraid to walk down the street because they know everybody on the block, and there's no reason to be afraid. . . . I think the

181

block association is great. It's like the
old New England meetings, where everybody
gets together. It is direct . . . a direct
responsibility for what is happening on
the block.

Not only does this Activist support his claims
by referring to personal experience, he also employs
an appeal to authority by "footnoting" expert com-
mentary on the situation. The Prospect-Lefferts-
Gardens Association has also been on the offensive
when it comes to the stigma of the neighborhood by
suggesting that an integrated neighborhood is better
than an all-white community! Some of those most
active in the organization speak of the many benefits
of living with many different ethnic and religious
groups, such as the exposure of children to multi-
cultural environments. Unfortunately, there are
very few white Americans for whom an integrated
community is a preferred residence. As noted
previously, even nonwhites see living side-by-side
with whites as a political necessity, and not as an
aesthetic preference.

Although there are many things that Activists
in the Lefferts Manor and Prospect-Lefferts-Gardens
engage in that are similar to those of community
groups in other less stigmatized locations, because
they share a common culture of community, the ultimate
goal of community projects here is somewhat different.
This is because in the inner city, community and
community respectability cannot be taken for granted.
Local residents cannot rely on the ability of the
casual observer to "see" community in their setting.
Practically, the aims of local Activists are to combat the stigma of the area in order to convince
stable middle-class families to remain, and to entice
suitable replacements for the Achievers who have
moved out of the neighborhood.

The ideal, normal American community is
organized, clean, beautiful, and has a venerable
history. Of course, the ideal American community is
also white, but Activists must be content with a
minimally integrated community. Activists plan
community events--meetings, street fairs, demonstrations, beautification and garden projects, and other
"normal" community happenings. They have a community
newspaper to spread the "good news" about the
neighborhood as a counterforce to the bad news that

is so much a part of city life, and city media. They research the history of the area, and seek out local notable residents to bring about proper recognition of the community. Who would expect that college presidents, professors, lawyers, doctors, city officials and businessmen live in a black neighborhood? All these things they do in the hope that their "significant others" will believe that their self-community is a desirable place to live.

The moral career of the Activist often takes on aspects of what Max Weber denoted as a "calling"; "as a matter of moral obligation."[33] When Activists engage in efforts to change the definition of their community from a negative to a positive one, they are put in "double jeopardy." Firstly, they are "discredited" because of their residence, and secondly, they are "discreditable" because they try to create appearances that normals do not expect from the stigmatized.[34] Activists' crusades can also create wide gulfs between themselves and those they purport to lead through the creation of "virtual" identities that are "out of character" and thereby convey to their neighbors a personal distaste for shared, "actual" identities.[35] In other words, their activities highlight local problems by publicly denigrating and rejecting them.

Implications and Applications

It was the purpose of this book to relate the personal troubles of inner-city residents to macro-logical problems and to demonstrate how individual quests for community are influenced by societal ideals and issues, such as rationalization of territory, disenchantment in the urban environment, racism, and the American culture of community. To understand the problems of inner-city residents a humanistic approach was offered which emphasized methodological and theoretical approaches found in symbolic interactionist and social constructionist analyses of society. These perspectives bring into sharper focus the interface of common human needs with larger issues. It is obvious that this work can only raise more questions than it either addresses or answers. It is hoped that those intrigued by the issues raised herein, attempt to employ the methods for urban analyses suggested in this book to study the residents of other troubled neighborhoods in other cities, and that these efforts will ultimately lead to a more humanistic urban social science and urban social policy.[36]

Although this book focuses, by necessity, on some of the special problems of nonwhite inner-city communities, the framework outlined of the community paradigm is applicable to other central city areas. White lower- and working-class communities in the city and suburbs are especially vulnerable to change, and, as shown by the history of the Lefferts Manor, suburbs have a tendency to become citified and then inherit all the typical urban ills. The community problems noted in Prospect-Lefferts-Gardens differ from other neighborhoods in degree, and not in essence.

In providing financial, social services and other aid to residents of the inner city, it is important to realize that these people live in a negatively defined social environment. This environment affects their self and group images, as well as their motivations and methods, for self and neighborhood improvement, when that opportunity arises. To some degree comprehensive and lasting solutions to their problems require the upgrading of their situations, not only physically and objectively but symbolically and subjectively as well.

The majority of the people who reside in Prospect-Lefferts-Gardens and other city neighborhoods are not poor and disadvantaged objectively, yet they suffer because their community has been stigmatized. One need only to magnify the problems of these people several times in order to understand what people who live in "actual" low-income and minority ghettoes (including public low-income housing projects) suffer due to their locations. "Problem" families and individuals need residential stability. Their constant relocation creates enormous problems for children, for example, and are required to make new friends at every stop along the way to nowhere. The stigma of their neighborhoods also reduces the desire of people to make lasting friends and neighbors who are important for day-to-day living among the poor. Given the stigma of some local neighborhoods, it is not surprising that frequently in such areas, despite ethnic and class homogeneity, there is little social

184

solidarity such as was found in the traditional ethnic ghetto, as was noted by Louis Wirth in his study of the Jewish ghetto.[37] People are not planning to stay in the area but are hoping to move away from it. One does not build personal and family ties to a neighbor who is seen as "undesirable."

Low-income housing is _ipso facto_ stigmatized and undesirable for those who live in it, as well as for those outside. The constant failures of low-income housing projects in cities, and also in the suburbs, vividly testifies to the lack of concern that residents have for what outsiders believe they should be "grateful." Living in low-income housing projects is a constant reminder of failure in society. The institutional look of most projects, even if brand new and innovatively designed, cannot hide the fact that they were built for those who could not "make it" on their own. The general stigma of public assistance, then, has an environmental corollary. Familiarity with the ideas presented in these pages should be helpful to practitioners who are often faced with the apathy or hostility of low-income, or minority groups toward their local environment. They cannot be expected to take pride in an enclave that has been defined and labelled as a "community of failures."[38]

Also, others who are similarly trapped in residences such as nursing homes and orphanages can be expected to have equivalent negative reactions and attitudes toward their physical and social surroundings.[39] It is only the defeated person who does not try to escape from his or her prison, or does not try to destroy it. The effectiveness of half-way houses and other "community facilities" should be carefully reconsidered in light of the ideas presented here. It does little good to provide community-based residential facilities or treatment centers in already stigmatized areas. And one should realize that the facilities themselves are stigma for those who use them, and for those who live nearby. It is quite understandable, therefore, that residents who think well of their neighborhood will fight against the "invasion" of social service centers into their community space.

It is through an understanding of the social-psychology of community activists that new hope for the preservation of modern cities is found. Their

moral career, or "calling," is a natural outcome
given that they must constantly justify to themselves
and others the moral value of their inner-city
community existence. In a way their activities are
"rituals" in the same sense that Fustel de Coulanges
outlined the rites and rituals associated with the
founding and maintenance of ancient cities.

Many of the things that Activists do today
can be favorably compared to those of the leaders
of ancient cities. The ancient city venerated its
past and maintained holy relics of founders in
central places of worship to demonstrate continuity
of sacred inhabitance. Activists in the Lefferts
Manor and Prospect-Lefferts-Gardens worked hard to
obtain an Historical Landmarks designation for the
Manor, a public expression of respect for the
hallowed history of the community. The designated
area is shown in Map 14. The designation, in effect,
"beatifies" part of the neighborhood and prevents
people from desecrating it. Even the belief that
the ancients and primitive people in general have
about the power of name symbolism has its modern
counterpart. As noted in earlier chapters, neighborhood names often convey symbolic contents.
Places like Bedford-Stuyvesant and Brownsville have
definite "bad magic" associated with them. Prospect-
Lefferts-Gardens Activists created their own new
name to counter the stigma of Crown Heights, which
during the 1960s began to obtain an undesirable
reputation; Prospect comes from Prospect Park,
Lefferts is borrowed from the elite Lefferts Manor,
and Gardens from the nearby Botanical Gardens. Parks
and gardens give rise to positive images in the mind.
Other neighborhoods in Brooklyn have similarly
developed new names to combat stigma and attract
newcomers. This is a reminder of the names chosen
for suburban communities in the 1950s. Every place
in suburbia was a "town" or "village," and the
streets were christened "drives," "lanes," and
"paths" of marigolds, roses and elms. For the
Prospect-Lefferts-Gardens Activist, the name allows
them to psychologically separate themselves from
the residents of nearby less fortunate areas. These
symbolic changes, and other activities in the
community, have at least altered the official neighborhood maps of the city, although it remains to be
seen whether they will change the mental maps of all
of the city's residents.

Map 14. HISTORICAL LANDMARKS DISTRICT, 1978.

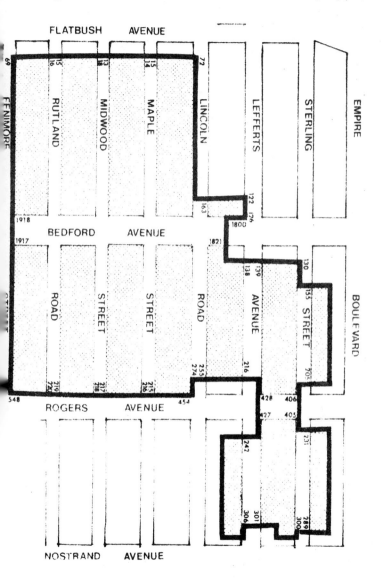

The aim of this book has not been to offer easy solutions to urban problems, but to stimulate research and debate. Ultimately the stereotypes of the inner-city and minority group communities must be changed via the judicious use of the media and educational institutions, as well as solving the "real problems" of crime and deterioration. Otherwise, the self-fulfilling prophecy of racial and ethnic change, and inevitable decay of city neighborhoods, will continue to operate to the detriment of the poor, the near-poor, and also the middle class. If unchecked, the processes may turn whole cities into "communities of failures."

NOTES

Chapter I

[1] For the social and physical structure of cities in history
see: de Coulanges (1975), Mumford (1961), Pirenne (1956),
Sjoberg (1960), Adna Weber (1963) and Max Weber (1958).

[2] For criticisms of urban renewal and related programs
see: Frieden and Morris (1968), Gans (1968), Greer (1965),
Lupo et al. (1971), Norwood (1974), Piven and Cloward (1971)
and Bellush and Hausknecht (1971).

[3] For an interesting discussion of the roots of the
"anti-urban bias" in Victorian England (which had a great
impact on American urban planning) see: Glass (1968). See
also Gist and Fava (1975:573-95) for negative images of
city, as well as Spengler (1928:85-186).

[4] For a good start on a re-emphasis on the social-
psychology of urban life see Karp et al. (1971). See also
Douglas (1970).

[5] Other succession, and ethnic urban dweller, studies
are: Conot (1974), Cayton and Drake (1945), Glazer and
Moynihan (1963), Grodzins (1958), Handlin (1959), Hoover and
Vernon (1959:chap. 9), Kramer and Leventman (1961), Northwood
and Barth (1965) and Strauss (1970).

[6] Firey (1947) and Suttles (1972:chap. 2). See also
Hunter (1974), Lynch (1960) and Strauss (1969) for important
ideas on the symbolic basis of city life.

[7] For generally unfavorable discussions of qualitative
studies and methodology see: Huber (1973), Lazarsfeld and
Barton (1955), and Lofland (1974). For criticism of modern
sociology's over-reliance on quantitative methods see: Coser
(1975) and Timasheff (1955:321). See Phillips (1973) for
criticism of over-reliance on methodology in social science,
and Glazer and Strauss for innovative qualitative methods.

[8] For examples, and discussion, of micro-sociology in
various forms see: Birenbaum and Sagarin (1973), Douglas
(1970), Garfinkle (1967), Mehan and Wood (1975) and Psathas
(1973). Lyman and Scott argue in their Sociology of the
Absurd: "The term 'absurd' captures the fundamental assumption
of this new wave: The world is essentially without meaning. In

contrast to that sociology which seeks to discover the real meaning of action--a sociological reality, such as the functional meaning of social behavior--this new sociology asserts that all systems of belief, including that of the conventional sociologist, is arbitrary. The problems previously supposed to be those of the sociologists are in fact the everyday problems of the ordinary man. It is he that must carve out meanings in a world that is meaningless. Alienation and insecurity are fundamental conditions of life--though they are experienced differently by individuals and groups--and the regular rehumanization of man is everyman's task" (1970:1).

[9] For alineation in the modern world and urban environment see: Baltzell (1969), Faris and Dunham (1939), Freud (1930), Fromm (1941), Durkheim (1947, 1951), Janowitz (1952), Lofland (1973), Marx (1964:167-77), Packard (1972), Reich (1970), Riesman (1950), Simmel (1950:402-24), Stein (1960) and Weber (1964).

[10] For interesting discussions of the relationship between biological and cultural forces in social life see: Van den Berghe (1974) and Suttles (1972:16-18). Suttles (1972: chaps. 5, 6 and 7) provides criticism of these approaches to the social, but Gould (1974) is most devastating. For basis of bio-social approach see: Ardrey (1961), Hall (1966), Lorenz (1966), Lyman and Scott (1967), Morris (1967, 1969) and Wilson (1975). Relatedly see: Milgram (1974) and Skinner (1972).

[11] Clark (1947, 1950, 1965). See also Fanon (1967).

[12] For more on black community life see: Du Bois (1899), Frazier (1957), Johnson (1968) and Osofsky (1966).

[13] For a novel on the Amboy Dukes of Brownsville in the 1940s see Schulman (1950). See also Yablonski (1963) and Thrasher (1927) for sociological discussions of gangs and turf.

[14] Bellush and David (1971), Connery (1968), Conot (1967), Hayden (1967) and Oppenheimer (1969) are excellent additions to Kerner (1968) and Skolnick (1969) on riots.

[15] See especially Banfield (1974) and Grodzins (1959).

[16] Northwood and Barth (1965).

[17] For "tipping point" see: Wolf (1967, 1968). Relatedly see Deutsch and Collins (1951).

[18] See: Erbe (1975), Gossett (1963), Allport (1954), McCord et al. (1969), Myrdal (1944), Riemers (1972) and Sheatsley (1966).

[19] Thomlinson notes: "Whether the minority be defined by religion, race or nationality; whether the city be in Asia, Europe, or the United States; or whether the group segregated be composed of complete 'pariahs' or merely 'social inferiors' --some degree of physical separation is practiced more or less everywhere" (1969:13). He also notes, "Climbing into the upper brackets does not remove a Negro from the prospect of residential segregation, for high-status Negroes often have their own 'gilded ghettoes" (1969:14). For other works on ethnic, racial and economic segregation see: Molotsch (1969), Willie (1975) and Wolf et al. (1967).

[20] For important works on the social self see: Deutsch and Krauss (1965:173-216), Cooley (1956), Lindesmith and Strauss (1977), Mead (1934), Reynolds (1970) and Rose (1972). Two good steps in the direction of bringing together the self and the environment are Bell and Tyrwhitt (1972) and Proshansky et al. (1970). See also Zeisel (1975).

[21] See Goffman (1959) for ideas on human activity as "performances" which will be employed throughout this work. See also Goffman (1963).

[22] For more on ethnic neighborhoods and social mobility and assimilation see: Feldstein (1974), Gans (1962), Ianni (1957), Keller (1968), Liebow (1967), Lewis (1966), Kramer and Leventman (1961), Podhertz (1967), Riis (1968), Smith (1943), Schoenfeld (1969), Suttles (1968), Ware (1965) and Wirth (1928). See also Berry and Horton (1974:chap. 11).

[23] Suttles uses cognitive maps in reference to the total city: "There is the cognitive map which residents have for describing, not only what their city is like but what they think it ought to be like. This cognitive map of the city need not necessarily correspond closely with the actual physical structure" (1972:22). Anselm Strauss, similarly, and previously, discussed the cognitive structure of the city. In his work he used the term "orbits." The term refers to meanings assigned to space, which have an effect on social and economic activity (1969). See also: Lee (1968), Lynch and Rivkin (1970), Gould and White (1974), Proshansky (1970) and Von Uexkuell (1957).

[24] See also Blumer (1969) for basics of Symbolic-interaction approach, as well as Hewitt (1976).

191

[25] For housing mobility studies related to status see: Back (1962), Rossi (1955) and Rubin et al. (1969).

[26] For basis of idea of cognitive balance and dissonance see Festinger (1962) and Heider (1946, 1958). Cognitive balance and dissonance are particularly important concepts in understanding the pressure to adjust one's self and community image in order for them to "fit" each other.

[27] See Kierkegaard (1962). For more on existentialism see also Langiulli (1971).

[28] This problem of bias toward upper-class and otherwise elite historical landmarks has been taken up by the New York City Landmarks Preservation Committee, and they are now considering designating monuments, or sites, of working-class contributions to the city. See Gans (1974) for discussion of class and taste.

[29] For the early history of Brownsville see Landesman (1970).

Chapter II

[1] Shane Stevens, "Instant Urban Renewal," New York Times, June 19, 1971.

[2] "Dim Future for City if White Exodus Continues," Daily News, February 25, 1975.

[3] "Middle-class Whites: A New Minority?" Sunday News, March 2, 1975.

[4] "A Plan to Halt White Flight," New York Post, February 25, 1975.

[5] In 1978 CPD was split in two. Prospect-Lefferts-Gardens became part of CPD-9.

[6] For analysis of New York City decentralization see: Ravitch (1972), Berube and Gittell (1969), Katznelson (1973) and Altschuler (1970).

[7] Plan for Neighborhood Government for New York City (New York: City Planning Commission, 1970), p. 4.

[8] Champ Strategy, City of New York Document NYCPC 72-04 (New York: City Planning Commission, 1972), pp. 68-69.

[9] *Historic and Beautiful Brooklyn* (Brooklyn, NY: Brooklyn Eagle, 1947), p. 1.

[10] See Keller (1968:19-86) for extensive discussion of neighboring activities in different kinds of neighborhoods.

[11] For Simmel on Sociability" see (1950:40-57).

[12] Wirth (1938).

[13] See: Coleman (1957), Dobriner (1958), Gans (1967), Seeley et al. (1956) and Whyte (1956) for oft-cited suburban studies.

[14] For an insightful analysis of the impact of prison on self identity see Irwin (1970). See also Glaser (1964) and Sykes (1958).

[15] Clark (1965) and Wirth (1928).

[16] John L. Hess, "Snobbery About One's Address Remains Alive in City," *New York Times*, January 4, 1974, p. 3. See also Form and Stone (1957) and Clark and Cadwallader (1973).

Chapter III

[1] *Lefferts Manor Brochure* (Brooklyn, NY: Lefferts Manor Association, 1938), pp. 11-12.

[2] See Kotler (1969) for an extensive discussion of the process by which American cities have expanded at the expense of nearby communities.

[3] Jacobs (1961:379-81).

[4] Unless otherwise noted, all newspaper articles quoted from are taken from the *Brooklyn Eagle*.

[5] For politics of confrontation see: Boskin and Rosenstone 1972), Howard (1974), Kerner (1968), Marx (1971), Skolnick 1969), and Vickers (1975).

[6] Peter Frieberg, "A Fine Neighborhood in Prospect," *New York Post*, February 27, 1974.

[7] *Lefferts Manor Brochure* (Brooklyn, NY: Lefferts Manor Association, 1938).

[8]"Your Key to the Lefferts Manor Association" (Brooklyn: Lefferts Manor Association, n.d.).

Chapter IV

[1]Suburbs have often been referred to as dormitory communities, reflecting the separation between home and work place. One often forgets that cities have many neighborhoods which are exclusively residential, and that people leave them during the day to go to work.

[2]See especially Gans (1967) for a criticism of the myth of suburbia and its people.

[3]Most writings on cities and towns have noted some physical boundary that separates the more affluent from the less affluent neighborhoods. Where such physical boundaries, e.g., railroad tracks, highways, etc., do not exist one can rely on such methods as those developed by Shevky and Bell (1955).

[4]Frazier (1962).

[5]Sol Yurick, New York Times, July 1, 1972.

[6]"Study Finds Suburbanites Displacing Poor in Cities," New York Times, August 2, 1978.

[7]Suttles (1972:chap. 2).

Chapter V

[1]For intensive treatments of housing and landlords see: Sternlieb (1966), Back (1962) and Burchell and Sternlieb (1973).

[2]See Goffman (1959:142-65) for analyses of various types of secrets. The "open" secret in Goffman's schema can become a "dark" secret when disclosure would heavily damage the holder. For example, Manor covenant violations are "open" secrets in the company of other Manorites, but "dark" in the presence of outsiders.

[3]See Janowitz (1952) for origination of the concept of "limited liability." See also Greer (1962).

[4]For a discussion of "virtual" versus "actual" identities see Goffman (1963:1-40).

[5] The "backstage," according to Goffman, is the area in which players can be themselves, because it is out of the view of audiences. The backstage is also the place where planning of performances and routines takes place (1959:112).

Chapter VI

[1] See Schutz (1964:107-11) for a discussion of the relationship between home and community of space, intimacy and face-to-face interaction.

[2] Weber (1964:123).

[3] Goffman (1963:4).

[4] Wirth (1928) and Clark (1965).

[5] Irwin (1970) analyzes the impact of the prison environment of the self-identity of criminals.

[6] Cooper (1974). For self-residential relations see also: Form and Stone (1957), Schorr (1970:320-32) and Suttles (1972:35), as well as Wertheim (1968).

[7] Baltzell (1967), Nisbet (1953) and Warren (1971).

[8] Warren (1971:247).

[9] Dennis (1968). See also Schrag (1975).

[10] Krase (1973, 1974).

[11] See Glass (1968) for discussion of anti-urban bias.

[12] Merton (1968:441-74).

[13] For studies of Bedford-Stuyvesant see Connolly (1977) and Manoni (1973).

[14] Gold (1952).

[15] Every year in New York City, civil rights and other organizations issue reports demonstrating the neglect of non-white areas. For discussions of New York's problems see also: Bellush and David (1971), Connery and Caraley (1969) and Gottehrer (1965).

[16] For biases of planners, see especially Gans (1968) and Jacobs (1961).

[17]Some of the reasons for the persistence of traditional ethnic neighborhoods have been noted by: Gans (1962), Suttles (1972), Bradburn et al. (1971), Hunter (1974) and Wirth (1928).

[18]For the un-Americanized ethnic, the neighborhood of birth continues to be focal, and reference, point for social and cultural life. In many ethnic communities the first and second generation continue to use English as the "second" language, although fluency in English has been reached.

[19]My own observations of many Brooklyn neighborhoods indicate that a missing cohort in changing neighborhoods is the 19-25 age group. New communities tend to be young; deteriorated neighborhoods have a high proportion of elderly; and changing neighborhoods are, so to speak, middle-aged. For a poignant essay on being "Left Behind in Brooklyn" see Levine (1972).

[20]Since the mid-1960s the arsonist profile has changed from that of a psychopath to either a landlord or a tenant. Both set fires for economic gain. See Barracato and Michelmore (1976) for extensive discussion of arson.

[21]See: Clark and Cadwallader (1973), Helmer and Eddington (1970), Hershberger (1974), Lewin (1951), Lee (1970), Lynch (1970), Proshansky (1970), Schorr (1970) and Strauss (1970).

[22]For a basic discussion of signs and symbols see Lindesmith and Strauss (1956:53-58). Most social-psychologists argue that a symbol is a sign that has a meaning arrived at by convention.

[23]See Oppenheimer (1969:54-55) for a discussion of the idealization of peasant life by intellectuals.

[24]See Chinoy (1955) for an often referred to treatment of the American Dream. See also Sennett and Cobb (1972) for the reaction of working-class people to the realization of their "failure" in American society.

[25]Self-flagellation has a long history among religious fanatics, who feel that self-punishment and self-denial are ways to atone for past and future transgressions. My own observations seem to indicate that self-abuse (verbal) is almost "expected" of social failures.

[26]Gans (1962:31).

[27]People whom I have observed moving out of the neighbor-hood are as enthusiastic about their new home as are religious converts about their new religion.

[28]Merton (1968:185-248) encompasses the complete discussion of Merton's paradigm of "Social Structure and Anomie."

[29]See Zablocki (1973) for a study of such an alternative community form. See Kephart for text on "Extraordinary Groups" (1976).

[30]For a discussion of "traps" as related to Goffman's notions of the "discredited" and the "discreditable" see Goffman (1963:3-5).

[31]For examples of the range of definitions and conceptu-alizations of "community" by "experts" see: Bernard (1973: 3-35), Hillery (1955) and Minar and Greer (1968).

[32]See Gans (1962:28-32) for his four major "behavior styles," which include "routine seekers" and "middle-class mobiles."

[33]For Weber's "calling" see (1963:33 and 81; 1958:79-92).

[34]Goffman defines "appearances" as "those stimuli which function at the time to tell us of the performer's social statuses" (1959:24). For "discredited" and "discreditable" see (1963:3-5).

[35]See Goffman (1963:2-3) for definitions of "actual" and "virtual" social identities.

[36]A most recent discussion of what is meant by "humanist" sociology is given by McLung-Lee (1973). Two good examples of humanist approaches to policy-related disciplines are Friedmann (1973) and Leff (1978). See also Mumford (1968) and Goodman (1947) for earlier examples.

[37]Wirth (1928) noted that although the Jews were stigmatized by their ghetto residence it was also a source for positive social and psychological identities.

[38]For studies of the effect of living in low-income neighborhoods see: Freid and Gleicher (1961), Lewis (1966) and Schorr (1966). See especially Rainwater (1970) for a study of the ill-fated Igo-Pruitt housing project in St. Louis and Dorman (1972). For "Stigma of Poverty" see Waxman (1977).

[39]See, for example, Goffman (1961) and Stephens (1975) on asylums and single room occupancy hotels respectively.

SELECTED BIBLIOGRAPHY

.llport, Gordon
1954   The Nature of Prejudice. Cambridge, Mass.: Addison-
        Wesley.

ltschuler, Alan
1970   Community Control. New York: Frederick A. Praeger.

rdrey, Robert
1961   The Territorial Imperative. New York: Atheneum.

rensberg, Conrad M., and Solon T. Kimball
1965   Culture and Community. New York: Harcourt, Brace and
        World.

ack, Kenneth
1962   Slums, Projects and People. Durham, N.C.: Duke
        University Press.

altzell, Digby E. (ed.)
1967   The Search for Community in Modern America. New York:
        Harper and Row.

anfield, Edward C.
1974   The Unheavenly City Revisited. Boston: Little,
        Brown and Company.

arracato, John, and Peter Michelmore
1976   Arson! New York: W.W. Norton and Company.

arton, Allen H., and Paul F. Lazarsfeld
1955   "Some Functions of Qualitative Research in Social
        Research," Bobbs-Merrill Reprint S-336. From the
        Frankfurter Beiträge zur Soziologie, Band 1, 1955.

ell, Gwen, and Jacqueline Tyrwhitt (eds.)
1972.   Human Identity in the Urban Environment. Baltimore:
        Penguin Books.

ell, Wendell, and Marion D. Boat
1957   "Urban Neighborhoods and Informal Social Relation-
        ships," American Journal of Sociology 62:391-98.

ellush, Jewel, and Stephen M. David (eds.)
1974   Race and Politics in New York City. New York:
        Frederick A. Praeger.

Bellush, Jewel, and Murray Hausknecht
1971   Urban Renewal: People, Politics and Planning.   New
        York: Doubleday-Anchor.

Becker, Ernest
1973   The Denial of Death.   New York: The Free Press.

Berger, Bennet M.
1960   Working Class Suburb.   Berkeley: University of
        California Press.

Bernard, Jesse
1973   The Sociology of Community.   Glenview, Ill.: Scott,
        Foresman and Company.

Berry, Brian J.L., and Frank Horton
1970   Geographic Perspectives on Urban Systems.   Englewood
        Cliffs, N.J.: Prentice-Hall.

Berube, Maurice R., and Marilyn Gittell
1969   Confrontation at Ocean-Hill Brownsville.   New York:
        Frederick A. Praeger.

Birenbaum, Arnold, and Edward Sagarin (eds.)
1973   People in Places: The Sociology of the Familiar.
        New York: Frederick A. Praeger.

Blonsky, Lawrence
1975   "The Desire of Elderly Nonresidents to Live in a Senior
        Citizens' Apartment Building," Gerontologist 15:88-91.

Blumer, Herbert
1969   Symbolic Interaction: Perspective and Method.   Engle-
        wood Cliffs, N.J.: Prentice-Hall.

Boskin, Joseph, and Robert A. Rosenstone (eds.)
1972   Season of Rebellion.   New York: Holt, Rinehart and
        Winston.

Bradburn, Norman M., Seymour Ludman and Galen L. Gockel
1971   Side by Side: Integrated Neighborhoods in America.
        Chicago: Quadrangle Books.

Butler, Robert N.
1975   Why Survive? Being Old in America.   New York: Harper
        and Row.

Burchell, Robert W. and George Sternlieb
1973   Residential Abandonment: The Tenement Landlord
        Revisited.   New Brunswick: New Jersey Center for
        Urban Policy Research.

Carp, Frances M.
    1975   "Ego Defense or Cognitive Consistency Effects in
            Environmental Evaluations," Journal of Gerontology
            30:707-11.

Cassirer, Ernst
    1944   An Essay on Man. New Haven: Yale University Press.

CHAMP Facts
    1972   Crown Heights Area Maintenance Program. New York:
            Department of City Planning, 72-06.

CHAMP Strategy
    1972   Crown Heights Area Maintenance Program. New York:
            Department of City Planning, 72-04.

Chinoy, Ely
    1955   Automobile Workers and the American Dream. New York:
            Doubleday and Company.

Cicourel, Aaron
    1964   Method and Measurement in Sociology. New York: The
            Free Press of Glencoe.

Clark, Kenneth B.
    1950   "Emotional Factors in Racial Identification and
            Preference in Negro Children," Journal of Negro
            Education 19:341-50.

Clark, Kenneth B.
    1965   The Dark Ghetto: Dilemmas of Social Power. New York:
            Harper and Row.

Clark, Kenneth B. and M.K. Clark
    1947   "Racial Identification and Preference in Negro
            Children," in Readings in Social Psychology, eds.
            T.M. Newcomb and E.L. Hartley. New York: Holt.

Clark, W.A.V. and M. Cadwallader
    1973   "Residential Preferences: An Alternative View of
            Inter-Urban Space," Environment and Planning 5:
            693-705.

Coleman, James S.
    1957   Community Conflict. New York: The Free Press.

Connery, Robert H. (ed.)
    1968   Urban Riots. New York: Vintage Books.

Connery, Robert H. and Demetrious Caraley
  1969   Governing the City. New York: Frederick A. Praeger.

Connolly, Harold X.
  1977   A Ghetto Grows in Brooklyn. New York: New York
         University Press.

Conot, Robert
  1967   Rivers of Blood, Years of Darkness. New York: Bantam
         Books.

Conot, Robert
  1974   American Odyssey. New York: Morrow.

Cooley, Charles H.
  1956   Human Nature and the Social Order. Glencoe: The Free
         Press of Glencoe.

Cooper, Clare
  1974   "The House as a Symbol of Self." In Designing for
         Human Behavior. Edited by Jon Lang, Charles Burnette,
         Walter Moleski and David Vachon. Stroudsberg, Pa.:
         Dowden, Hutchinson and Ross Incoporated, pp. 130-46.

Coser, Lewis A.
  1975   "Presidential Address: Two Methods in Search of a
         Substance," American Sociological Review 40:691-700.

Day, Clarence
  1969   "Father's Home Disappears." In City Life. Edited
         by Oscar Schoenfeld and Helen MacLean. New York:
         Frederick Praeger, pp. 73-79.

De Coulanges, Fustel N.D.
  1975   The Ancient City. Garden City: Doubleday and Company.
         Translated by Willard Small. (Originally published
         in 1893.)

Dennis, N.
  1968   "The Popularity of the Neighborhood Community Idea."
         In Readings in Urban Sociology. Edited by R.E. Pahl.
         New York: Pergamon Press, pp. 74-92.

Deutsch, Morton and Mary E. Collins
  1951   Interracial Housing. Minneapolis: University of
         Minnesota Press.

Deutsch, Morton and Robert M. Kramer
  1965   Theories in Social Psychology. New York: Basic
         Books.

exter, Lewis A.
 1970   Elite and Specialized Interviewing. Evanston, Ill.:
        Northwestern University Press.

obriner, William M. (ed.)
 1958   The Suburban Community. New York: G.P. Putnam's Sons.

ollard, John
 1949   Caste and Class in a Southern Town. Garden City:
        Doubleday-Anchor.

orman, Michael
 1972   The Making of a Slum: How a Respectable Neighborhood
        Becomes an Urban Jungle. New York: Delacorte Press.

ouglas, Jack D. (ed.)
 1970   The Relevance of Sociology. New York: Appleton
        Century Crofts.

rake, St. Clair and Horace R. Cayton
 1945   Black Metropolis: A Study of Negro Life in a Northern
        City. New York: Harcourt, Brace and Janowitz.

u Bois, W.E.B.
 1899   The Philadelphia Negro. Philadelphia: University of
        Pennsylvania Press.

uncan, High Dalziel
 1969   Symbols and Social Theory. New York: Oxford University
        Press.

uncan, Otis D. and Beverly Duncan
 1957   The Negro Population of Chicago. Chicago: University
        of Chicago Press.

urkheim, Emile
 1947   The Division of Labor in Society. Glencoe: The Free
        Press. Translated by George Simpson.

urkheim, Emile
 1951   Suicide. New York: The Free Press.

rbe, Briggette Mach
 1975   "Race and Socioeconomic Segregation," American
        Sociological Review 40:801-12.

anon, Frantz
 1967   Black Face, White Masks. New York: Grove Press.
        Translated by Charles Lam Markmann.

Faris, Robert and H. Warren Dunham
    1939   Mental Disorders in Urban Areas. Chicago: University
            of Chicago Press.

Feldstein, Stanley and Lawrence Costello (eds.)
    1974   The Ordeal of Assimilation. Garden City: Anchor Press.

Festinger, Leon
    1962   A Theory of Cognitive Dissonance. Stanford: Stanford
            University Press.

Firey, Walter
    1945   "Sentiment and Symbolism as Ecological Variables,"
            American Sociological Review 10:140-48.

Firey, Walter
    1947   Land Use in Central Boston. Cambridge: Harvard
            University Press.

Form, William H. and Gregory Stone
    1957   "Urbanism, Anonymity and Status Symbolism," American
            Journal of Sociology 63:502-14.

Frazier, E. Franklin
    1962   Black Bourgeoisie. New York: Collier.

Frazier, E. Franklin
    1932   The Negro Family in Chicago. Chicago: University of
            Chicago Press.

Freud, Sigmund
    1939   Civilization and Its Discontents. London: Hogarth
            Press.

Fried, Marc and Peggy Gleicher
    1961   "Some Sources of Residential Satisfaction in an Urban
            Slum," Journal of the American Institute of Planners
            27:305-15.

Frieden, Bernard and Robert Morris
    1968   Urban Planning and Social Policy. New York: Basic
            Books.

Friedman, John
    1973   Retracking America: A Theory of Transactive Planning.
            Garden City: Anchor Press.

Fromm, Erich
    1941   Escape from Freedom. New York: Farrer and Rinehart.

Gans, Herbert
  1961   The Urban Villagers.   New York: The Free Press of
          Glencoe.

Gans, Herbert
  1967   The Levittowners.   New York: Vintage Books.

Gans, Herbert
  1968   People and Plans.   New York: Basic Books.

Gans, Herbert
  1974   Popular Culture and High Culture: An Analysis and
          Evaluation of Taste.   New York: Basic Books.

Garfinkel, Harold
  1967   Studies in Ethnomethodology.   Englewood Cliffs, N.J.:
          Prentice-Hall.

Gist, Noel P. and Silvia Fleiss Fava.
  1975   Urban Society.   Sixth edition.   New York: Thomas Y.
          Crowell.

Glaser, Barney G. and Anselm L. Strauss
  1967   The Discovery of Grounded Theory.   Chicago: Aldine
          Publishing Company.

Glaser, Daniel
  1964   The Effectiveness of a Prison and Parole System.   New
          York: Bobbs-Merrill Company.

Glass, Ruth
  1968   "Urban Sociology in Great Britain."   In Readings in
          Urban Sociology.   Edited by R.E. Pahl.   New York:
          Pergamon Press, pp. 47-73.

Glazer, Nathan and Daniel P. Moynihan
  1963   Beyond the Melting Pot.   Cambridge: M.I.T. and
          Harvard University Press.

Goffman, Erving
  1961   Asylums.   Garden City: Doubleday and Company.

Goffman, Erving
  1959   The Presentation of Self in Everyday Life.   Garden
          City: Doubleday and Company.

Goffman, Erving
  1963   Stigma.   Englewood Cliffs, N.J.: Prentice-Hall.

Goffman, Erving
1963   Behavior in Public Places. Glencoe: The Free Press.

Gold, Ray
1952   "Janitors versus Tenants: A Status Income Dilemma,"
        American Journal of Sociology 57:486-93.

Goldstein, Leon J.
1965   "The Phenomenological and Naturalistic Approaches to
        the Social." In The Philosophy of the Social Sciences.
        Edited by Maurice Natanson. New York: Random House,
        pp. 286-301.

Goodman, Paul and Percival Goodman
1947   Communitas. Chicago: University of Chicago Press.

Gossett, Thomas F.
1963   Race: The History of an Idea in America. Dallas:
        Doubleday.

Gottehrer, Barry
1965   New York City in Crisis. New York: Pocket Books.

Gould, Peter and Rodney White
1974   Mental Maps. Baltimore: Penguin Books.

Gould, Stephen Jay
1974   "The Nonscience of Human Nature," Natural History
        83:24-29.

Green, Gerald
1956   The Last Angry Man. New York: Scribner.

Greer, Scott
1962   The Emerging City. New York: The Free Press.

Greer, Scott
1965   Urban Renewal and American Cities. Indianapolis:
        Bobbs-Merrill Company.

Grodzins, Morton
1958   The Metropolitan Area as a Racial Problem. Pittsburgh:
        University of Pittsburgh Press.

Gutman, Robert and David Popenoe (eds.)
1970   Neighborhood, City and Metropolis. New York: Random
        House.

Gutman, Robert
1972   People and Buildings. New York: Basic Books.

206

Hall, Edward
    1966   The Hidden Dimension. Garden City: Doubleday.

Handlin, Oscar
    1959   The Newcomers: Negroes and Puerto Ricans in a Changing
            Metropolis. Garden City: Doubleday-Anchor.

Hawley, Amos H.
    1971   Urban Society: An Ecological Approach. New York:
            Ronald Press.

Hayden, Tom
    1967   Rebellion in Newark. New York: Random House.

Heider, Fritz
    1946   "Attitudes and Cognitive Organization," Journal of
            Psychology 21:107-12.

Heider, Fritz
    1958   The Psychology of Interpersonal Relations. New York:
            John Wiley and Sons.

Helmer, John and Neil A. Eddington
    1970   Urbanman: The Psychology of Urban Survival. New
            York: The Free Press..

Hershberger, Robert G.
    1974   "Predicting the Meaning of Architecture," In Designing
            for Human Behavior. Edited by Jon Lang, Charles
            Burnette, Walter Moleski and David Vachon. Stroudsberg,
            Pa.: Dowden, Hutchinson and Ross Incorporated, pp.
            147-56.

Hewitt, John P.
    1976   Self and Society: A Symbolic Interactionist Social
            Psychology. Boston: Allyn Bacon.

Hillery, George A. Jr.
    1955   "Definitions of Community: Areas of Agreement," Rural
            Sociology 20:192-204.

Hobson, Laura
    1947   Gentleman's Agreement. New York: Simon and Schuster.

Hochschild, Arlie Russell
    1973   The Unexpected Community. Englewood Cliffs, N.J.:
            Prentice-Hall.

Hoover, Edgar and Raymond Vernon
    1959   Anatomy of a Metropolis. Cambridge: Harvard University
            Press.

207

Howard, John
1974   The Cutting Edge. Philadelphia: J.B. Lippincott.

Huber, Joan
1973   "Symbolic Interaction as a Pragmatic Perspective:
        The Bias of an Emergent Theory," American Socio-
        logical Review 38:274-84.

Hunter, Albert
1974   Symbolic Communities: The Persistence and Change of
        Chicago's Local Communities. Chicago: University of
        Chicago Press.

Ianni, Francis A.J.
1957   "Residential Mobility and Occupational Mobility as
        Indices of Acculturation of Ethnic Groups," Social
        Forces 36:

Irwin, John
1970   The Felon. Englewood Cliffs, N.J.: Prentice-Hall.

Jacobs, Harriet
1970   "The Journalistic and Sociological Enterprises as
        Ideal Types," American Sociologist 5:348-50.

Jacobs, Jane
1961   The Death and Life of Great American Cities. New
        York: Random House.

Janowitz, Morris
1952   The Community Press in the Urban Setting. New York:
        The Free Press of Glencoe.

Johnson, James Weldon
1968   Black Manhattan. New York: Atheneum.

Jones, Robert W.
1961   "A Note on Phases of the Community Role of the Par-
        ticipant Observer," American Sociological Review
        26:446-50.

Karp, David A., Gregory P. Stone and William C. Yoels
1977   Being Urban: A Social Psychological View of Urban
        Life. Lexington, Ky.: D.C. Heath.

Katznelson, Ira
1973   "Urban Counterrevolution." In 1984 Revisited:
        Prospects for American Politics. New York: Alfred
        Knopf, pp. 139-64.

Keller, Suzanne
  1968   The Urban Neighborhood. New York: Random House.

Kephart, William M.
  1976   Extraordinary Groups. New York: St. Martin's Press.

Kerner, Otto
  1968   Report of the National Advisory Commission on Civil
         Disorders. New York: Bantam Books.

Kierkegaarde, Søren
  1962   Philosophical Fragments. Translated by D. Swenson.
         Princeton: Princeton University Press.

Kotler, Milton
  1969   Neighborhood Government. New York: Bobbs-Merrill
         Company.

Kramer, Judith, and Seymour Leventman
  1961   Children of the Gilded Ghetto. New Haven: Yale
         University Press.

Krase, Jerome
  1973   The Presentation of Community in Urban Society.
         Ann Arbor: University Microfilms, 74-1916.

Krase, Jerome
  1974   "Toward a Phenomenological View of Community
         Organization." Paper presented at the Eastern
         Sociological Society Annual Meetings, Philadelphia.

Krase, Jerome
  1977   "Reactions to the Stigmata of Inner City Living."
         Journal of Sociology and Social Welfare 4:997-1011.

Krase, Jerome
  1979   "Community in the Inner City as a Moral Problem."
         Humanity and Society 3:35-52.

Krase, Jerome
  1979   "Stigmatized Places-Stigmatized People: Crown Heights
         and Prospect-Lefferts-Gardens." In Brooklyn USA: The
         Fourth Largest City in America. Edited by Rita
         Seiden-Miller. New York: Brooklyn College Press and
         Columbia University Press, pp. 251-62.

Landesmann, Alter L.
  1970   A History of New Lots, Brooklyn, including the Villages
         of East New York, Cypress Hills and Brownville. Port
         Washington, N.Y.: Kennikat Press.

Lang, Jon, Charles Burnette, Walter Moleski and David Vachon
    1974   Designing for Human Behavior. Stroudsberg, Pa.:
           Dowden, Hutchinson and Ross Incorporated.

Langiulli, Nino (ed.)
    1971   The Existentialist Tradition. Garden City: Doubleday
           and Company.

Lauer, Robert H., and Warren H. Handel
    1977   Social Psychology: The Theory and Application of
           Symbolic Interactionism. Boston: Houghton Mifflin.

Lee, Alfred McClung
    1973   Toward Humanist Sociology. Englewood Cliffs, N.J.:
           Prentice-Hall.

Lee, Terence
    1970   "Urban Neighborhood as a Socio-Spatial Schema." In
           Environmental Psychology: Man and His Physical Setting.
           Edited by Harold M. Proshansky, William H. Ittelson
           and Leanne G. Rivlin. New York: Holt, Rinehart and
           Winston, pp. 349-69.

Leff, Herbert L.
    1978   Experience, Environment and Human Potentials. New
           York: Oxford University Press.

Leibowitz, Barry
    1975   "Age and Fearfulness: Personal and Situational
           Factors." Journal of Gerontology 30:696-700.

Levine, Ralph
    1972   "Left Behind in Brooklyn." In Nation of Nations.
           Edited by Peter I. Rose. New York: Random House,
           pp. 335-46.

Lewin, Kurt
    1951   Field Theory in Social Science. New York: Harper
           and Brothers.

Lewis, Oscar
    1966   La Vida. New York: Random House.

Liebow, Elliot
    1967   Tally's Corner. Boston: Little, Brown and Company.

Lindesmith, Alfred, and Anselm L. Strauss
    1956   Social Psychology. New York: Holt, Rinehart and
           Winston.

Lofland, John
1974   "Styles of Reporting Qualitative Field Research."
       The American Sociologist 9:101-11.

Lorenz, Konrad
1966   On Aggression. New York: Harcourt, Brace and World.

Lupo. Alan, Frank Colcord and Edmund P. Fowler
1971   Rites of Way. Boston: Little, Brown and Company.

Lyford, Joseph P.
1966   The Airtight Cage. New York: Harper and Row.

Lyman, Stanford M., and Marvin B. Scott
1967   "Territoriality: A Neglected Sociological Dimension."
       Social Problems 15:236-49.

Lynch, Kevin
1960   The Images of the City. Cambridge: MIT and Harvard
       University Press.

Lynch, Kevin, and Malcolm Rivkin
1970   "A Walk around the Block." In Environmental Psychology:
       Man and His Physical Setting. Edited by Harold M.
       Proshansky, William H. Ittelson and Leanne G. Rivlin.
       New York: Holt, Rinehart and Winston, pp. 631-42.

Lynd, Robert S., and Helen My Lynd
1920   Middletown. New York: Harcourt, Brace and World.

Malcolm X
1964   The Autobiography of Malcolm X. New York: Grove Press.

Marx, Gary T. (ed.)
1971   Racial Conflict. Boston: Little, Brown and Company.

Marx, Karl
1956   Karl Marx: Selected Writings in Sociology and Social
       Philosophy. New York: McGraw-Hill. Translated
       and edited by T.B. Bottomore.

Manoni, Mary H.
1973   Bedford Stuyvesant. New York: Quadrangle Books.

McCord, William, John Howard, Bernard Friedberg and
Edwin Harwood
1969   Life Styles in the Black Ghetto. New York: W.W.
       Norton and Company.

Mead, George Herbert
1934   Mind, Self and Society. Chicago: University of
        Chicago Press.

Mehan, Hugh, and Houston Wood
1975   The Reality of Ethnomethodology. New York: John
        Wiley and Sons.

Merton, Robert K.
1968   Social Theory and Social Structure. New York: The
        Free Press.

Milgram, Stanley
1974   Obedience to Authority. New York: Harper and Row.

Mills, C. Wright
1959   The Sociological Imagination. New York: Oxford
        University Press.

Minar, David, and Scott Greer
1969   The Concept of Community. Chicago: Aldine
        Publishing Company.

Molotsch, Harvey L.
1969   "Racial Change in a Stable Community." American
        Journal of Sociology 75:226-38.

Morris, Desmond
1967   The Naked Ape. New York: Dell Publishing Company.

Morris, Desmond
1969   The Human Zoo. New York: McGraw-Hill.

Mumford, Lewis
1938   The Culture of Cities. New York: Harcourt, Brace
        and World.

Myrdal, Gunnar
1944   An American Dilemma. 2 vols. New York: Harper and
        Brothers.

Natanson, Maurice (ed.)
1965   The Philosophy of the Social Sciences. New York:
        Random House.

Newman, Oscar
1972   Defensible Space. New York: Macmillan.

Nisbet, Robert A.
  1953   The Quest for Community. New York: Oxford University
          Press.

Northwood, L.K., and A.T. Barth
  1965   Urban Desegregation: Negro Pioneers and their White
          Neighbors. Seattle: University of Washington Press.

Norwood, Christopher
  1974   About Paterson. New York: Harper and Row.

Oppenheimer, Martin
  1969   The Urban Guerilla. Chicago: Quadrangle Books.

Osofsky, Gilbert
  1966   Harlem: The Making of a Ghetto. New York: Harper
          and Row.

Packard, Vance O.
  1972   A Nation of Strangers. New York: McKay.

Pahl, R.E. (ed.)
  1968   Readings in Urban Sociology. New York: Pergamon Press.

Park, Robert E.
  1952   Human Communities. Glencoe: The Free Press.

Park, Robert E.
  1966   The City. Chicago: University of Chicago Press.

Phillips, Derek L.
  1973   Abandoning Method. San Francisco: Jossey-Bass.

Pirenne, Henri
  1956   Medieval Cities. Garden City: Doubleday-Anchor.
          Translated by Frank Halsey.

Piven, Frances Fox, and Richard A. Cloward
  1971   Regulating the Poor. New York: Pantheon Books.

Podhertz, Norman
  1967   Making It. New York: Random House.

Proshansky, Harold M., William H. Ittelson and
Leanne G. Rivlin (eds.)
  1970   Environmental Psychology: Man and His Physical Setting.
          New York: Holt, Rinehart and Winston.

Psathas, George (ed.)
    1973   Phenomenological Sociology. New York: John Wiley and
            Sons.

Rainwater, Lee
    1970   Behind Ghetto Walls. Chicago: Aldine Publishing
            Company.

Ravitch, Diane
    1972   "Community Control Revisted." Commentary 53:69-74.

Reich, Charles A.
    1970   The Greening of America. New York: Bantam Books.

Reynolds, Larry, and Janice M. Reynolds (eds.)
    1970   The Sociology of Sociology. New York: David McKay.

Reynolds, Larry, Ted R. Vaughn, Janice M. Reynolds and
    Leon Warshay
    1970   "The Self in Symbolic Interaction Theory." In The
            Sociology of Sociology. Edited by Larry and Janice M.
            Reynolds. New York: David McKay, pp. 422-38.

Riis, Jacob
    1968   Jacob Riis Revisited. Garden City: Doubleday-Anchor.
            Edited by Francesco Cordasco.

Rose, Arnold M.
    1962   "A Systematic Theory of Symbolic Interaction." In
            Human Behavior and Social Processes. Edited by
            Arnold M. Rose. Boston: Houghton Mifflin, pp. 3-19.

Rose, Arnold M. (ed.)
    1962   Human Behavior and Social Processes. Boston:
            Houghton Mifflin.

Rose, Peter I.
    1972   Seeing Ourselves. New York: Alfred A. Knopf.

Rose, Peter I. (ed.)
    1972   Nation of Nations. New York: Random House.

Rossi, Peter H.
    1955   Why Families Move. Glencoe: The Free Press.

Schoenfeld, Oscar, and Helen MacLean (eds.)
    1969   City Life. New York: Frederick Praeger.

214

Schorr, Alvin
1970   "Housing and Its Effects." In Environmental
        Psychology: Man and His Physical Setting. Edited by
        Harold M. Proshansky, William H. Ittelson and Leanne
        G. Rivlin. New York: Holt, Rinehart and Winston,
        pp. 319-33.

Schrag, Peter
1970   "Is Main Street Still There?" Saturday Review,
        January 17, 1970.

Schulman, Irving
1950   Amboy Dukes. New York: Pocket Books.

Schutz, Alfred
1964   Collected Papers II: Studies in Social Theory. The
        Hague: Martinus Nijhoff.

Seeley, John R., R. Alexander Sims and Elizabeth W. Loosely
1956   Crestwood Heights. Toronto: University of Toronto
        Press.

Selby, Hubert
1964   Last Exit to Brooklyn. New York: Grove Press.

Sennett, Richard, and Jonathan Cobb
1972   The Hidden Injuries of Class. New York: Alfred A.
        Knopf.

Sheatsley, Leon
1966   "White Attitudes toward Negroes," Daedalus 44:217-29.

Shevky, Eshref, and Wendell Bell
1955   Social Area Analysis. Stanford: Stanford University
        Press.

Shibutani, Yamatsu
1966   Improvised News. Indianapolis: Bobbs-Merrill Company.

Simmel, Georg
1950   The Sociology of Georg Simmel. London: The Free Press.
        Translated and edited by Kurt Wolff.

Sjoberg, Gideon
1960   The Preindustrial City. New York: The Free Press.

Skinner, B.F.
1971   Beyond Freedom and Dignity. New York: Alfred A. Knopf.

215

Skolnick, Jerome
  1969   The Politics of Protest. New York: Ballantine Books.

Smith, Betty
  1943   A Tree Grows in Brooklyn. New York: Harper.

Sommer, Robert
  1969   Personal Space: The Behavioral Basis of Design.
         Englewood Cliffs, N.J.: Prentice-Hall.

Spengler, Oswald
  1928   The Decline of the West, Volume II. New York:
         Alfred A. Knopf. Translated by Charles A.A. Atkinson.

Stanforth, Deidre, and Martha Stamm
  1972   Buying and Renovating a House in the City. New York:
         Alfred A. Knopf.

Stea, David
  1970   "Space, Territory and Human Movements." In Environ-
         mental Psychology: Man and His Physical Setting.
         Edited by Harold M. Proshansky, William H. Ittelson
         and Leanne G. Rivlin. New York: Holt, Rinehart and
         Winston, pp. 37-42.

Stein, Maurice
  1960   Eclipse of Community. New York: Harper and Row.

Stephens, Joyce
  1975   "Society of the Alone: Freedom, Privacy and
         Utilitarianism as Dominant Norms in the SRO,"
         Journal of Gerontology 30:230-35.

Sternlieb, George
  1966   Tenement Landlord. New Brunswick, N.J.: Rutgers
         University Press.

Stonequist, E.V.
  1937   Marginal Man. New York: Charles Scribner's Sons.

Strauss, Anselm
  1969   Images of American Cities. New York: The Free Press.

Strauss, Anselm
  1970   "Life Styles and Urban Space." In Environmental
         Psychology: Man and His Physical Setting. Edited by
         Harold M. Proshansky, William H. Ittelson and Leanne
         G. Rivlin. New York: Holt, Rinehart and Winston,
         pp. 303-12.

Suttles, Gerald D.
   1968   The Social Order of the Slum. Chicago: University
          of Chicago Press.

Suttles, Gerald D.
   1972   The Social Construction of Communities. Chicago:
          University of Chicago Press.

Sykes, Gresham
   1958   Society of Captives. Princton: Princeton University
          Press.

Taeuberg, Carl E., and Alma F. Taeuber
   1969   Negroes in Cities. New York: Atheneum.

Thrasher, Frederick
   1927   The Gang. Chicago: University of Chicago Press.

Timasheff, Nicholas S.
   1955   Sociological Theory. New York: Random House.

Van den Verghe, Pierre L.
   1974   "Bringing the Beasts Back In: Toward a Biosocial
          Theory of Aggression," American Sociological Review
          39:778-88.

Van den Berghe, Pierre L.
   1975   Man in Society: A Biosocial View. New York: Elsevier
          Press.

Veblen, Thorsten
   1912   Theory of the Leisure Class. New York: Macmillan.

Vickers, George
   1975   The Formation of the New Left. Lexington, Mass.:
          D.C. Heath.

Von Uexkuell, Jacob
   1957   "A Stroll Through the Worlds of Animals and Men."
          In Instinctive Behavior. Edited by Claire H.
          Schiller. New York: International University Press.

Ware, Caroline
   1965   Greenwich Village 1920-30. New York: Harper and Row.

Warren, Roland L.
   1971   Truth, Love and Social Change. Chicago: Rand McNally.

Warren, Roland L.
  1972   The Community in American Society. Second edition.
         New York: Rand McNally.

Waxman, Chaim I.
  1977   The Stigma of Poverty. Elmsford, N.Y.: Pergamon
         Press.

Weaver, Robert C.
  1966   The Urban Complex. Garden City: Anchor Books.

Webb, Eugene, Dorothy T. Campbell, Richard D. Schwartz and
  Lee Sechrest
  1966   Unobtrusive Measures in the Social Sciences. Chicago:
         Rand McNally.

Weber, Adna
  1963   The Growth of Cities in the 19th Century. Ithaca,
         N.Y.: Cornell University Press.

Weber, Max
  1958   The Protestant Ethic and the Spirit of Capitalism.
         New York: Charles Scribner's Sons. Translated by
         Talcott Parsons.

Weber, Max
  1958   The City. New York: The Free Press. Translated by
         Don Martindale and Gertrud Neuwirth.

Weber, Max
  1964   The Theory of Economic and Social Organization. New
         York: The Free Press. Translated and edited by
         Talcott Parsons. Translated by A.M. Henderson.

Wertham, Carl
  1968   The Social Meaning of the Physical Environment.
         Unpublished Ph.D. dissertation. Berkeley: University
         of California.

Wharton, Edith
  1969   "A Little Girl's New York." In City Life. Edited by
         Oscar Schoenfeld and Helen McLean. New York:
         Frederick Praeger, pp. 59-72.

Whyte, William F.
  1943   Street Corner Society. Chicago: University of
         Chicago Press.

Whyte, William F.
  1956   Organization Man. New York: Simon and Schuster.

Wirth, Louis
  1928   The Ghetto. Chicago: University of Chicago Press.

Wilson, Edward O.
  1975   Sociobiology. Cambridge: Harvard University Press.

Wolf, Eleanor P.
  1968   "The Tipping Point in Racially Changing Neighborhoods."
          In Urban Planning and Social Policy. Edited by
          Bernard Frieden and Robert Morris. New York: Basic
          Books, pp. 149-55.

Wolf, Eleanor P., and Charles Lebeaux
  1967   "Class and Race in the Changing City: Searching for
          New Approaches to Old Problems." In Social Science
          and the City. Edited by Leo F. Schnore. New York:
          Praeger.

Wolf, Robert P.
  1973   1984 Revisited: Prospects for American Politics.
          New York: Alfred A. Knopf.

Yablonsky, Lewis
  1963   The Violent Gang. New York: Macmillan.

Zablocki, Benjamin
  1973   The Joyful Community. Baltimore: Penguin Books.

Zeisel, John
  1975   Sociology and Architectural Design. New York:
          Russell Sage Foundation.

DATE DUE